THINKING
a b o u t
JUDAISM

THINKING
a b o u t
JUDAISM

Philosophical Reflections on Jewish Thought

Sheva Grumer Brun

JASON ARONSON INC.
Northvale, New Jersey
Jerusalem

The author gratefully acknowledges permission to quote from the following source:

TANAKH: A New Translation of The Holy Scriptures According to the Traditional Hebrew Text (JPS: Philadelphia 1985).

This book was set in 11 pt. Weiss by Hightech Data Inc., of Bangalore, India, and printed and bound by Book-mart Press, Inc. of North Bergen, NJ.

Library of Congress Cataloging-in-Publication Data

Brun, Sheva Grumer, 1935–
    Thinking about Judaism : philosophical reflections on Jewish thought / by Sheva
    Grumer Brun.
        p. cm.
    Includes bibliographical references and index.
    ISBN 0–7657–6037–1
    1. Judaism. 2. Philosophy, Jewish. 3. Philosophy, Modern—
Influence. I. Title
BM565.B86 1998
296—DC21   98–38765

Printed in the United States of America on acid-free paper. For information and catalog write to Jason Aronson Inc., 230 Livingston Street, Northvale, NJ 07647-1726, or visit our website: www.aronson.com

CONTENTS

Contents

Contents

PREFACE

*T*hinking about Judaism examines the light shed by philosophy upon variegated areas of Jewish life and academic studies, such as Jewish history, Jewish ethics, Jewish law, and Jewish aesthetics. The teachings of leading theorists on the subjects of general history, ethics, law, and aesthetics inspire us to think about the corresponding teachings in Judaica. The book contains not only the thoughts of world philosophers, but also, and primarily, the teachings of many leading Jewish thinkers on the subjects at hand. Space is devoted to such ancient Jewish luminaries as Rabbi Saadia Gaon and Maimonides and to recent teachers such as Rabbi Joseph B. Soloveitchik, Professor Abraham Joshua Heschel, and Rabbi Yitzchok Hutner, among other well known cerebral and sensitive personalities.

The book commences with a brief introduction illustrating how philosophy can solve or dissolve many hotly debated discussions carried on by both philosophers and the rest of us. Several examples of actual Jewish debates that evaporate in the face of philosophical inspection are given. With this introduction serving as a background, Jewish history, ethics, law, education, religion, aesthetics, and social thought are expounded upon in a philosophical manner. As is typical of philosophical discourse, some subjects are probed in an analytical fashion, and others presented with a broad panoramic view. Sometimes the tree and its roots are dissected and at other times we view the magnificent forest. Although the book is largely a work of philosophy, the presentation is in a popular manner. Anyone may enjoy reading it.

The subject matter contained herein has been addressed only sporadically in the past and not heretofore in book form. Anyone who enjoys speculation and values philosophy will discover much material over which to ponder. One who loves reading about Jewish subjects will savor a varied and delicious menu from which to choose. Finally, one who is attracted simultaneously to philosophy and Judaica will find both food for thought and genuine Jewish *nachas* (delight).

Ideally a literary enterprise of this nature should be undertaken by a philosopher who is at the same time a specialist in Judaic studies, and who also is associated with academia, where relevant matters are discussed and debated among colleagues and students. Since the present writer possesses none of these qualifications, an explanation for taking on this task is in order.

This type of study or philosophical investigation has not previously been undertaken and the author feels that the pursuit is a worthwhile one. With the realization that this writing is not the consummate or final work in the field, Rabbi Tarfon's advice was heeded: "You are not called upon to complete the work, yet you are not free to desist from it."[1] It is also believed that the reader will appreciate the ideas of the thinkers and philosophers who are frequently quoted or briefly expounded upon throughout. Some of their cited thoughts are not presently available in English and thus their appearance here might be of some benefit. The author of the *Netivot HaMishpat*, Rabbi Yaakov of Lissa (c. 1760–1832), wrote that if a book has one good idea in it, it is redeemed.[2] With the citation of many ideas from various great thinkers, the book should have at least some redeeming quality.

It is obvious that the various chapters herein are of markedly different lengths and of different quality. This is so for a number of reasons that include the nature of the subjects themselves, the literature available on them, the author's own knowledge or lack of knowledge in different areas, and also her subjective predilections for some subjects over others.

Mention should be made that some of the longer footnotes in the book are not merely bibliographical references to the material in the text proper. They contain thoughts that are relevant to the discussion in the text and supplement it.

The author hopes that the reader will find the application of general philosophy to the various areas of Jewish studies and thought to be an intellectually rewarding pursuit. She also wishes to express appreciation and gratitude to teachers, family, and friends from whom she has learned and continues to learn. Any errors in that learning, whether manifest in this book or not, are her sole responsibility and not theirs.

The author would like to take this opportunity to thank Production Editor Kenneth J. Silver, Copy Editor Robert Crowder, and the entire Jason Aronson Inc. staff for their help and input in producing this book.

ENDNOTES

1. Avot 2:16.

2. Rabbi Jacob of Lissa (Lorbeerbaum), introduction to *Torat Gittin*. See also Hanoch Teller, *The Story of the Steipler Gaon*, (Brooklyn, New York: Mesorah Publications, 1986), p. 58. I thank my son for locating the *Torat Gittin* source for me.

ONE

JEWISH PHILOSOPHY

INTRODUCTION

I n introducing our subject, it is helpful to offer a few illustrations drawn
from general philosophy that contribute useful insights when we think
about matters of Jewish content. Ideas and concepts emanating from
the world of philosophy can illuminate Jewish intellectual discourse and
some of the topics discussed in later chapters.

The American philosopher William James wrote that during a camp-
ing party in the mountains he encountered a "ferocious metaphysical
dispute" centering around a squirrel. The squirrel was on the trunk of a
tree, running around it. A man was also running around the tree at the
same velocity as the squirrel. During the racing activity, the man and
the squirrel were always at equal distance from each other. The question
ferociously debated was whether or not the man actually went around
the squirrel. Some hotly argued that since the man ran around the entire
tree and the squirrel was on that tree, he automatically also ran around the
squirrel. Others just as heatedly insisted that since the man and the squirrel
were always equidistant from each other, the man obviously did not run
around the squirrel even if he ran around the tree. A problem similar to
the one presented by James is whether a person standing in one place is

moving or not, since the earth upon which he or she stands is actually in motion.

William James believed that problems of this sort can be solved or dissolved by determining what the arguing disputants *mean* by the words they utilize. "Which party is right," he wrote, "depends on what you *practically mean* by 'going round' the squirrel."[1] Along this line of thought Professor Martin Lean[2] used to claim as his postulate that "Words don't mean, people mean." Words are neutral, and the meaning they have derives from that which is given to them by the people who use them. This is reminiscent of the Biblical view that the animals were named by Adam, and their names are not God given.[3]

Metaphysical disputes like the one involving the squirrel are frequently encountered in heated debates on Jewish themes. People have argued that living in the Land of Israel in a secular, unredeemed state is tantamount to being in exile. Others retort that living in the Land of Israel is by definition contrary to being in exile. This issue can be debated ad nauseam without resolution. However, once it is realized that the debate is not about concepts, but rather how people are using them, the entire burning issue evaporates into thin air.

Another example of this type of philosophical disagreement is one side claiming that Jewish philosophy (or Jewish art, for that matter)[4] consists of philosophy related to something of Jewish interest;[5] another maintaining that the creator of the philosophy must be Jewish even if he or she deals with non-Jewish subjects;[6] and a third arguing vehemently that Jewish philosophy has to be both created by a Jew and possess Jewish content. The ferocity of this dispute vanishes when we apply the Jamesian solution of *practical meaning* to the argumentative situation. What is meant by Jewish philosophy is not something determined "out there," but is decided upon by the human beings who discourse on the subject.

Very illuminating on the subject of definition and meaning are the insights offered by Ludwig Wittgenstein, whose paternal grandfather was a convert from Judaism to Protestantism. He proclaimed that words and concepts do not lend themselves to simple definition. He illustrated this with the word "games." There is nothing in common, he maintained, between all games. There are card games, board games such as chess and checkers, ball games, the ring-a-ring-a-roses game, etc., but there is no common property shared by all of these. There are only family resemblances between them, a network of similarities overlapping and criss-crossing. To explain to another person what a game is, we should describe games and perhaps also add, "This and similar things are called 'games.'" Wittgenstein believed that there are no clear cut boundaries distinguishing between different concepts to be defined.[7] According to him, definition is to be understood in terms of usage. "The meaning of a word is its use in the language."[8]

Let us apply this thesis of Wittgenstein to an actual discussion overheard on the topic, What (or who) is a rabbi? An individual was referred to as "Rabbi So-and-So." Someone quickly countered that he is no rabbi. It is true that he was ordained, but he does not make a living within any Jewish field. If his method of livelihood is derived from outside the Jewish community with no relationship to anything Jewish, why should he receive the appellation of rabbi? The dispute continued with the counterattack that since the man was ordained, he deserves and should be called rabbi, the presupposition being that ordination alone is sufficient to endow one with the right to the rabbinic title. As a corollary to this lively discussion, two other de facto uses of the word rabbi will be cited. Hebrew school teachers are frequently called rabbis, even though they may not have been ordained. Also, some erudite talmudic scholars, regardless of their occupations, are referred to as rabbis on the basis of their extensive knowledge, with or without their having received ordination. It becomes clear from the foregoing that like the word "game" for Wittgenstein, the word "rabbi" is fluid, and there are no specific lines of demarcation between the various usages of the terminology involved. Once this is realized, such debates as "Who is a rabbi?" take on a different perspective. We could say perhaps that such discussions are really not about the *cheftza* or object discussed, but rather more about the *gavra* or persons participating in the argumentation.

FALLACIES IN LOGIC

Before we proceed with the ensuing chapters, a few words should be devoted to the topic of "fallacies" in logic. As a logical term, a fallacy is "an invalid argument," [9] "a violation of a logical principle . . . a mistake in reasoning." [10] An interesting characteristic of fallacies is that they sometimes go unnoticed in the reasoning process because they are psychologically persuasive, [11] even if they have no logical validity. Although there are many kinds of logical fallacies, they are usually divided into two basic types: formal and informal fallacies.

The two fallacies we shall briefly examine are informal ones. The first one is called the *post hoc ergo propter hoc* or false cause fallacy. [12] We know that in the Middle Ages a large number of Jews in France and Germany gave up their lives rather than convert to the dominant Christian religion, while in Spain many Jews converted or became Marranos (pseudo-Christians). An argument given was that the latter converted more readily because they were influenced by their knowledge of secular studies whereas the former were entirely immersed in Talmudic or Rabbinic studies and therefore were more pious. To counteract this explanation, some speculated that the Iberian Jews were more wealthy than their Ashkenazic counterparts and therefore perhaps hung onto life more tenaciously rather than surrender it. [13] It is not always easy to ferret out what brings on events, and one must not arrive at causal conclusions hastily just because one event immediately follows upon another and on the surface seems causally related.

The second fallacy to be dealt with is the *argumentum ad hominem*. This fallacy is divided into two different types. The first is "abusive" in that the one who commits it denigrates the person with whom he or she is arguing. That individual will be called wicked, stupid, or ignorant, and therefore his or her claims have no validity. "Instead of trying to *disprove the truth* of what is asserted, one attacks the man who made the assertion." [14] We constantly see, hear, and read in the Jewish press about vitriolic personal attacks upon ideological opponents. This rancor is persuasive propaganda, but nevertheless it is poor logic.

8

The second type of *argumentum ad hominem* is "circumstantial."[15] In this instance person A argues that what person B is affirming contradicts what he or she maintained elsewhere or in the past. Therefore, what is asserted now is not correct. In Hebrew dialectic, this is often referred to as *LiShitato*, meaning that one's current assertion is contradictory to one's prior affirmation, and thus is untenable. The fallacy lies in that the past argument may be incorrect, and the present one true.

It is hoped that the insights from general philosophy contained in these few introductory remarks will be useful to Jewish thinking and will be helpful with the topics found in the remaining chapters.

ENDNOTES

1. William James, "What Pragmatism Means," chap. II in *Pragmatism: A New Name for Some Old Ways of Thinking* (New York: Longmans, Green & Co., 1907).

2. Professor Martin Lean taught philosophy at Brooklyn College.

3. Gen. 2:19–20.

4. Steven S. Schwarzschild, "Aesthetics," in *Contemporary Jewish Religious Thought*, ed. Arthur A. Cohen and Paul Mendes-Flohr (New York: Free Press, 1987), p. 1.

5. Hegel's treatment of Jewish history and Judaism is an example of philosophy on a Jewish theme written by a non-Jew. Another such instance is Jean-Paul Sartre's essay on anti-Semitism.

6. Samuel Alexander, Henri Bergson, and Edmund Husserl are Jewish philosophers who wrote on non-Jewish themes. Chief Rabbi Abraham Issac Kook (1865–1935) distinguished between great Jews and Jews who are great, the latter referring to noncommitted or nonpracticing Jews who make significant contributions to non-Jewish culture.

7. Ludwig Wittgenstein, *Philosophical Investigations* (New York: Macmillan, 1953), Sections 66–69.

8. Ibid., Section 43. For a philosophical discussion of the concept of definition, see Raziel Abelson, "Definition," in *The Encyclopedia of Philosophy*, vol. 2, ed. Paul Edwards (New York: Macmillan, 1967), pp. 314–324.

9. J. L. Mackie, "Fallacies," in *The Encyclopedia of Philosophy* vol 3, op. cit. p. 169.

10. L. Susan Stebbing, *Thinking to Some Purpose*, (Baltimore: Penguin, 1939), p. 157.

11. Irving M. Copi, *Introduction to Logic*, (New York: Macmillan, 1953), p. 50.

12. Ibid., p. 62.

13. For another explanation of the variant reactions of Sephardim and Ashkenazim to religious persecution, see Gerson D. Cohen, "Messianic Postures of Ashkenazim and Sephardim," reprinted in Gerson D. Cohen, *Studies in the Variety of Rabbinic Cultures*, (Philadelphia: Jewish Publication Society, 1991), pp. 289–294.

14. Copi, op. cit., p. 54.

15. Ibid., p. 55.

TWO

Jewish History

T he German philosopher Johann Herder referred to the history of the Jews as "the greatest poem of all time."[1] What is it about Jewish history that evoked this cordial statement by Herder? After all, most people extol and laud their own histories. The rabbis tell us that there are three kinds of favorable phenomena, one of which is the favor that people feel for the land that they inhabit[2]—and presumably also for their history. In what ways is Jewish history different that Herder singles it out from others?

UNIQUENESS OF JEWISH HISTORY

There are four qualities that distinguish Jewish history and make it remarkable. The first of these has been pointed out by the historian Simon Dubnow (1860–1943). Dubnow entitled his multivolume history of the Jews, *A World History of the Jewish People*, a *Weltgeschichte*. He has done so because of the unique spaciotemporal feature of Jewish history: (1) In time, it is almost as old as world history; (2) In space, it occupies almost all geographical areas of the inhabited earth.[3] Because of this space-time feature, Jewish history is a history within history. Its events transpire against the background of all the happenings of mankind.

The second unique trait of Jewish history is the apparent indestructibility of the Jewish people. The Jewish nation is similar to prime matter. All efforts to destroy it, from Haman to Hitler, not only failed but frequently converted it to new ebullient energy. There always were and still are those, even among the learned and enlightened, who begrudge the Jewish people their very existence. For example, the polymath historian Arnold Toynbee considered them merely a fossil.[4] Be that as it may, it seems the Jews are here to stay.

Third, Jewish history is sacred history. History, as will be explained shortly, deals with the human past. However, it is impossible to comprehend Jewish history without taking into account that Jews consider history a divine-human partnership. Even a secular historian or an atheist cannot understand the Jewish psyche or history of the Jews without recognizing that Jews, except for the more recent secular ones, consider their history in terms of the covenant assumption. This entails both God and man as the subjects of history. Judaism teaches that God created nature, whereas history is coauthored.

An interesting corollary to this theological conception of Jewish history concerns the frequently made accusation that contemporary journalists, Jewish and Gentile, religious and secular, have a double standard when reporting the news about Israel. Behavior considered normal for other political states is judged unethical for Israel, which receives the gibes and criticism all for itself. Why is this so? Aside from blatant Jew hatred, the theological nature of Jewish history is at least partly the cause of this double-standard journalism, even by secular reporters. Israel is associated with Jews and Judaism, with religion and ethics, and consequently with right and wrong.

The fourth distinguishing character of Jewish history has to do with the fact that it is a history of a people who had and still have an unusually great impact upon others. Western and Middle Eastern civilizations have taken much from Judaism. The Jewish religion, besides being professed by its adherents for several millennia, is the foundation of Christianity and Islam. The impact of the Jewish people even in our own times is evident by the fact that matters concerning Jews and Israel occupy an amount of space in the daily newspapers and in periodicals way out of proportion theoretically warranted by the small Jewish population in the world and by the tiny area occupied by the State of Israel.

NATURE OF HISTORY

The pursuit of philosophy goes back to the sixth century B.C.E., and one would expect that history, which deals with the activities of mankind, would have occupied philosophers ever since then. Actually this is not the case. Professor Morris Raphael Cohen wrote that the theory of history is "the most neglected province of philosophy."[5] The term "philosophy of history" itself was first used most probably by Voltaire,[6] who lived in the eighteenth century. There are several reasons for the late appearance and relative neglect of this subject. Philosophy is occupied with the timeless, history with the timely; philosophy with the general, history with the specific; philosophy with ultimate reality, and history with daily occurrence.

Another reason for the late appearance of the philosophy of history has to do with the late appearance of history itself as a discipline, a separate subject matter with its own methodology. Although historical writings from ancient times are found, it is only with the late eighteenth and nineteenth centuries that independent interest in historical studies per se grew rapidly.[7]

The Positivistic philosopher Auguste Comte believed that it is a fundamental law of human mentality that societies passed through three stages: the theological, the metaphysical, and the scientific. In the theological phase, the human mind accounts for events through the operation of spirits or a single spirit. In the metaphysical stage, spirits are replaced by abstract forces. In the scientific or positive phase, men record phenomena and state the laws that govern them.[8] It is undoubtedly correct to assert that in the past two hundred years, man entered an historical phase, where events and institutions have been explained historically. To understand something often requires a genetic explanation, a determination of how things originated and subsequently developed. This growth of history as an independent study, along with the historical method of thinking, and the philosophy of history have parallels in the growth and development of Jewish historical writing, also in the nineteenth century. Jewish historiography and historical thought developed (mainly) from the Jewish Science or *Wissenschaft* movement of the previous century and a half. It studied Jewish life, literature, and institutions from an historical point of view, and it is responsible for the first modern complete history of the Jews by Heinrich Graetz (1817–1891) and for the major philosophy of Jewish history that was expounded by Rabbi Nachman Krochmal (1785–1840).

What are the subjects and problems that concern the philosophy of history? This branch of philosophy like most others has a twofold character, in that it is analytic and speculative. The former analyzes historiography, clarifying the logical, conceptual, and epistemological aspects of what historians do. The latter endeavors to discover the meaning and significance of history itself.[9] Those who reject the speculative, metaphysical aspect of historical theory could still profitably engage in the analytical endeavor.[10]

The subjects covered by the philosophy of history include: What is history? Why should one study it? What is the task of the historian? What is the nature of historical knowledge and explanation? Are there historical laws? Does history have a pattern, a meaning, or a goal? What role do great men play in history? How would history have differed if only certain factors had been slightly different? Are there any lessons to be learned from history?

The word "history" is ambiguous. It has two basic meanings: It is the totality of the human past and it is also the study and narration of it.[11] This definition, however, is fraught with difficulties. The totality of the human past does not really have historical significance. "Nothing is more obvious than that all men and all events are not equally worth studying."[12] Who cares which brand of soap political leaders favor or which shoelace they tie first? Even if one were a *yente* par excellence, exceedingly curious about everything that previously has happened without missing out on an iota, this type of knowledge would be both not achievable and undesirable. Even though all human deeds are said to be re-corded in the heavenly ledgers,[13] certainly the documentary and physical remains from which we gather and study historical knowledge do not reveal to us the entire story, every single event out of the human past. Besides, forgetting nothing and remembering everything not only would be impossible, but is simply an outright curse.[14] Both on a personal and on a societal level, it is debatable which is worse: forgetting everything or remembering everything. A proper balance between remembering and forgetting is requisite for psychological sanity. Thus while it might be true that everything that happened in the human past is history, history usually refers to that aspect of the human past, and the study of that past, that has significance and is therefore worthy of being remembered. It becomes obvious that the task of the historian is not simply a "scissors and paste" affair,[15] where he merely gathers the pertinent documents and records all that he finds. The historian has to select what is worth re-membering from all the material and sources at his disposal.

What guides the historian in determining what is worth remember-ing, what is historically significant? Before answering this query, it should be kept in mind, as mentioned, that even the most erudite historian is not omniscient about all that transpired in the past. The physical and documentary data about the past, as well as about the present, are not complete, and the historian's study is naturally limited by the available, surviving evidence. It is also essential to realize that there are differences between the way the past actually occurred and the way it is remem-bered.[16] The former is analogous to the Kantian noumena, the thing-in-itself, which can never be known with certainty, and the latter with what Kant called phenomena, which are susceptible to human categories of understanding. This element of inherent skepticism that Kant found in the study of nature also has its counterpart in our knowledge of history. The historian cannot attain the goal set forth by Leopold von Ranke, the "Nestor of Historians," who wished to write history "as it actually happened."[17] The evidence from the past that is utilized by his-torians was usually recorded by untrained laymen, and who can attest to their objectivity, reliability, and truthfulness? Samuel Butler sarcastically observed, "God cannot alter the past; that is why He is obliged to connive the existence of historians."[18]

Even trained, professional observers of the present scene, including journalists, novelists, social scientists, and historians, often differ among themselves concerning what they observe and record. A number of people might perceive the identical object and witness the same event. However, their reports of what they perceived and witnessed are not necessarily congruous with each other. The historian obviously has to sift through all the available material, often like a detective,[19] to ascertain what is reliable, and afterwards use his or her training and good judgment to evaluate its historical significance. The historian's likes and dislikes, or sense of values, help him decide which aspects of his knowledge of the past are important enough to be included as history.

The spirit of the age in which the historian lives also influences his or her decisions regarding what kind of history to write, what to include, what to omit, and what to stress. Benedetto Croce stated, "Every true history is contemporary history."[20] History is written differently in different ages for diverse readers. Perhaps the contemporaneous significance of historical writing is similar to the variegated views of the Rouen Cathedral painted by Monet at different hours of the day under varying lighting and atmospheric conditions. History, like the Cathedral, seems to have divergent appearances and nuances depending upon the time it is studied or viewed.

Some historians oppose the opinion that history has to have contemporary relevance or meaning and seem to be enamored with the past for its own sake.[21] The historian Augustin Thierry wrote, "I noticed that history attracted me for its own sake, as a picture of past times, quite independently of the lessons I drew from it for the present."[22] Although historians may be interested in the past for its own sake (lishma), they are nevertheless products of their own time, and are surely influenced by the age in which they live. Furthermore, they write for the readers of their time, and consequently present the past in an interesting and meaningful manner for contemporary needs and preferences.

JEWISH HISTORIOGRAPHY

The Jewish historian naturally is also a product of his or her age. The Biblical historian, as would be expected, wrote history from a theological perspective. The Bible is a religious work, and the history recorded therein is religiously oriented. The secular histories mentioned in the Bible are no longer extant,[23] and perhaps that is no coincidence. Later on, with the loss of political independence and the great value and stress placed upon Jewish scholarship, Jewish historiography, especially in the Middle Ages, is preoccupied with recording the growth of tradition and rabbinic learning.[24] Medieval Jewish historians were also concerned with relating the sufferings and persecutions that befell the Jewish people.[25] However, a great deal of the medieval recounting of Jewish scholarship and suffering is of the nature of chronicle rather than of history. Croce offered some distinctions between history and chronicle. He cited "the close bond between events that there is in history and the disconnectedness that appears on the other hand in chronicle, the logical order of the first, the purely chronological order of the second, the penetration of the first into the core of events, and the limitation of the second to the superficial or external." Croce affirmed that there is a different spiritual attitude between them. "History," he asserted, "is living chronicle, chronicle is dead history; history is contemporary history, chronicle is past history."[26]

Heinrich Graetz, in the nineteenth century, composed the first complete Jewish history written by a Jew since Josephus authored the *Antiquities of the Jews* at the end of the first century C.E. Graetz did much original work in the field and also utilized what others had written.[27] By and large, his *History of the Jews*, converts the previous chronological treatment of Jewish learning and persecution to a history of the two.[28] Cecil Roth (1899–1970) described Graetz's history as one where intellectual history sometimes overwhelms political history entirely, and in the latter area, greater prominence is given to suffering than to achievement.[29] Meyer Waxman (1887–1969) agreed that Graetz gave preponderance to the description of the spiritual development of the Jewish people but maintained that actually follows logically from the nature of Jewish history.[30]

Frequently there is a discussion whether history is an art or a science. Waxman, using Thomas Carlyle's expression, referred to Graetz as both an artist and an artisan, gathering the facts and presenting them sympathetically and in a manner that attracts the reader.[31] Cecil Roth maintained that Graetz wrote in a "style that is sometimes of classical beauty."[32] Graetz, in the words of Gotthard Deutsch, "mastered most of the details while not losing sight of the whole. . . . This history of the Jews is not written by a cool observer, but by a warm hearted Jew."[33]

Several negative criticisms have been leveled at Graetz's history. They include: (1) Graetz lacked understanding of mystical forces and movements, such as Kabbala and hasidism. He despised these, and considered them a malignant growth in Judaism. (2) He was not acquainted with or not interested in the history of the Jews in Poland, Russia, and Turkey. (3) He expressed contempt bordering on hatred for "the fossilized Polish Talmudist." (4) He referred to Yiddish as ridiculous gibberish. (5) He neglected the social and economic aspects of Jewish life.[34]

While these criticisms of Graetz's *History* are undoubtedly valid and perhaps inexcusable, they appear as greater faults to us at present than they would have in Graetz's nineteenth-century Western Europe. The works of Martin Buber (1878–1965) and Gershom Scholem (1897–1982) have introduced to the western mind the beauty, value, and important role played by the mystical and hasidic movements in Jewish life. Prior to the contributions of these two scholars, extolling the Kabbala and hasidism would have been anomalous and alien in the rational, philosophical milieu in which Graetz and his readers existed. His neglect and probable distaste for East European Jewry is a reflection of the general attitude of German Jewry toward its eastern brethren. In American history, the Uptown Jews of German origin were not always especially thrilled about Lower East Side Jewish immigrants from Russia and Poland. As for Graetz's denigration of the Yiddish language, there still are Jews today who refer condescendingly to Yiddish as jargon. The point is that while the criticisms of Graetz's history are well grounded, we have to understand that they reflect a twentieth-century outlook on a nineteenth-century German Jewish historian and his intellectual environment. In other words, the critics of a later age want to clothe a person of a different era according to the fashions they admire. Sometimes the thought occurs: What will be the critical evaluation of Ashkenazic historical writing when a Sephardic historian appears on the scene and judges our neglect of Sephardic culture and history? The perfect history can be written only by God, for he is omniscient, objective, fair, and possesses the proper perspective and overview of everything that has transpired. He alone could write the standard, accepted, and best-selling history of all time.

In the twentieth century came Simon Dubnow of Russia, who contributed historical writing about the Jews of Eastern Europe, including the hasidic movement, besides composing his general Jewish *History*. A product of more recent times, he was influenced by the sociological thinking of the twentieth century and wrote a different type of Jewish history from the one composed by Graetz. Dubnow was a secularist who wanted to avoid writing history as *geistesgeschichte* and *leidensgeschichte*, as intellectual history and martyrology. He called for a sociological approach to Jewish history, maintaining that the Jews did not only think and suffer, but lived as a distinct social group under a variety of conditions. Therefore, the subject of his Jewish history is the Nation in its various aspects of existence, with the Jewish people, not Judaism, as the focal point. Besides the social factors and forces, Dubnow also emphasized economic factors, but treated the literary and cultural achievements of the people in a very cursory manner.[35] Haim Hillel Ben-Sasson wrote that, "In the writing of history, Dubnow preferred describing 'objective' processes and circumstances, based upon a study of detailed events, to the portrayal of personalities, their feelings, and desires."[36]

The preeminent historian Salo Baron (1895–1989) wrote *A Social and Religious History of the Jews*, delineating two aspects of Jewish history rather than its entirety. He followed Dubnow in his social approach and even more so relegated the "lachrymose"[37] to the background. As the title of his work indicates, he was also preoccupied with the religious and cultural achievements of the Jewish people. Dr. Arthur Hertzberg described Baron's emphasis "on the social history of the people, rather than the achievements of individual figures, on elements and areas of cross-fertilization between Jews and their environment, rather than on pogroms and suffering." Hertzberg noted that Baron recognized both the Land of Israel and the Diaspora as the centers of Jewish creativity, unlike the Diaspora-orientated Dubnow and the Israel-centered Ben Zion Dinur (1884–1973).[38]

The most extreme Zionist approach to Jewish history is found in the short story "The Sermon," by Haim Hazzaz (1942–1973). Yudka, a simple laborer and hero of the story, sermonizes on the nature of Jewish history. He states that he is opposed to the value of most of it, and has no respect for it. He is a denier of the Diaspora experience, of the suffering and culture it produced, and the redemption for which it always longed. He senses that Zionism is actually a revolt against Jewish Messianism,[39] and assaults the idea that Zionists can continue to be Jews.[40] "When Yudka announces that Jews have no history, he presupposes that to have a history, one must make it; that is a people must be a physically powerful, politically autonomous entity initiating action and determining its own destiny."[41]

This brief overview of some Jewish historical writing is meant to show that historiography itself has a history, the nature of which varies in different periods of time. It should be obvious now that there are fads and styles in historiography, and they do determine the nature and character of the history that is being written. History does have an element of contemporaneity.

Besides being influenced by the time in which he or she lives, the historian's objectivity is also impeded by other factors, such as who his or her teachers were and his or her personal preferences, economic and social background, religion, and philosophy. This does not imply that the historian merely indulges in a subjective flirtation with the past. There is a distinction between history and propaganda.[42] The historian is trained to acquire a scientific methodology that aims for objectivity, and there are many historical facts that are accepted by all historians. History is not merely conjecture, or personal predilection. "Nevertheless, there is without doubt some prima facie case for an ultimate historical skepticism." [43]

Morton White, formerly of Harvard University, defended the possibility of achieving historical objectivity. He affirmed that there is a fallacy "typical of the philosophy of history, the confusion between the psychology of historical interpretation and its logic." There is a fundamental difference between the process of discovering and the process of justifying historical knowledge. Subjective factors might influence the former. The latter, however, has to be submitted to objective tests and methods of confirmation. [44]

It is noteworthy to point out that in contradistinction to general historiography, Jewish historical writing evolved from a theological, cultural emphasis to a sociological, political one, with Yudka, in Hazzaz's story, emphasizing a political-military approach. In contrast, the historian James Harvey Robinson was dissatisfied with the conventional, general history that was taught in American schools, and advocated replacing it with "The New History." He opposed the exclusively political, constitutional, and military emphasis in historical study and wanted to accentuate the intellectual and social trends of particular eras. His history textbooks were intended to have a more popular appeal than the older history books that stressed political factors. Robinson was a highly effective teacher and influenced some of his graduate students to study intellectual history. [45] Thus the currents of Jewish and non-Jewish historical writing seem to be flowing in opposite directions.

The question arises: Why should one bother studying general or Jewish history? Perhaps it is better to let bygones be bygones, and devote our time to the present in which we live and to the future toward which we aspire? We shall see in a different chapter [46] that the medieval Jew did not place a premium on the study of history. Devoting oneself to historical studies, it was maintained, took valuable time away from concentrating on religious texts. History was to be read only for leisure or studied for moral uplift. Maimonides (1135–1204) considered it a "waste of time" to read profane history, although he himself possessed historical knowledge and offered historical explanations for several Biblical commandments, such as those pertaining to animal sacrifices.[47]

In modern times, history gained respectability both as a field of study and as a methodology for explanation and understanding, as discussed above. To comprehend something often entails knowing its background, origin, and development. Thus, history became a necessity for adequate understanding. Some people, like Thierry, are attracted to the study of the past for its own sake. Enjoyment of the learning provides its own justification. Others find history to be broadening in a similar manner as geography. Instead of taking a vacation trip to a different place, the student of history takes a journey to a different time. History broadens our outlook just as travel does. Fritz Stern noted that "the study of the past should be a liberating experience, one which tears them [the historian and reader] away from the parochialism of time and place and enlivens the imagination. Macaulay was right in comparing history to foreign travel."[48] Knowing the past also reveals to us who we are. Part of the essence of personhood is having a memory of our past.[49] A people that does not know its history is similar to a person without a memory. Both suffer an identity crisis. Friedrich Nietzsche expounded upon the value of "monumentalistic" history, which concentrates upon the heroes of the past. We can derive comfort and inspiration from them for they make manifest that man is capable of greatness.[50] The American poet Longfellow wrote:

> Lives of great men all remind us
> We can make our lives sublime,
> And, departing, leave behind us
> Footprints on the sands of time.[51]

LESSONS OF JEWISH HISTORY

A reason frequently offered for studying history is that man learns from the past. This proposition is debatable. Hegel, the great synthesizer of world history, is quoted as saying, "We learn from history that we do not learn from history." [52] George Bernard Shaw in a similar spirit stated, "If history repeats itself, and the unexpected always happens, how incapable must man be of learning from experience." [53] The opposite point of view is expressed by George Santayana, "Those who cannot remember the past are condemned to repeat it." [54]

Is it possible to learn from the Jewish past? Are there lessons to be derived from Jewish history? Can they guide us in planning for the future, to avoid repeating previous errors, and consequently live better and wiser lives?

The Bible teaches us two important and intricately related lessons concerning history, though they will be treated separately for our purpose. The Bible informs us that hearkening to the word of God leads to political and social success, and abandoning the Divine teaching brings on disasters of all sorts to the people. We learn this lesson poignantly in the *Tocheicha*, the list of "blessings and curses" that the Bible enumerates, corresponding to whether the people adhere to or disavow the commandments of the Torah. [55]

At this juncture, it is essential to distinguish between lessons *from* history and lessons *for* history. The Biblical list of "blessings and curses" was composed at the time of the origin of the Jewish people, and its words obviously cannot be lessons from history. Rather its exhortations are meant to provide solid advice and guidance, or lessons for the future. A large section of the Book of Judges provides both lessons from and lessons for history. A major theme of the book is to inform and admonish us that whenever the Hebrews abandon God, turn to idolatry, or do that which is "evil in the eyes of the Lord," God raises up an enemy against them. Then when the people cry out from oppression, God has mercy upon them and sends a Savior-Judge to the rescue. [56]

The second historical lesson that the Bible teaches is particularly associated with the prophets. A central message of the prophets is that social justice determines a people's prosperity, that ethics plays a causative role in history. Amos states that the Northern Kingdom of Israel will be punished "because they have sold for silver those whose cause was just, and the needy for a pair of sandals."[57] This quote perhaps appeared a gross exaggeration until the 1970s, when individuals and nations would (as they still do) sell their souls for a barrel of oil.

An obvious lesson to be learned from Jewish history is that life for the Jews living in the Diaspora constitutes a precarious existence. Even though there is no ironclad law that persecution and expulsion of Jews must occur in all the places where they reside, it nevertheless might be prudent for them not to make themselves very much at home while living in exile. It might not be necessary to possess a wandering stick, but it might be prudent to own a passport. This is not to say that life in Israel is the epitome of security. Insecurity is part of human existence both on the personal and collective levels. However, being on guard is a lesson a Jew can learn from the past of his or her people.

The Biblical scholar and historical theorist Yehezkel Kaufmann (1889–1963) believed that the fundamental conclusion or lesson to be drawn from all of Jewish history is that the Jewish people will continue to exist, even though individual Jews become assimilated. The Jewish people, he proclaimed, cannot achieve redemption through assimilation in exile. Only via national redemption in the Land of Israel can the Jew cease to be an alien.[58]

The philosophy of history asks what is the nature of historical knowledge and explanation? Is history a branch of science or is it a unique autonomous discipline? J. B. Bury, the editor of the Cambridge Ancient History volumes, in his "Inaugural Lecture" asserted, "History is a science, no less and no more."[59] The self-taught historian Thomas Buckle believed that history would become a true science if historians were to search for and discover the regularities of human actions. Buckle in his history aspired to collect a multitude of facts and to derive laws of history from them.[60] Of course, if a historian is capable of discovering historical laws, then he or she should, in the way a scientist does, be able to predict the future. In reality, historians generally do not indulge in attempts at predicting what will occur. It is said instead that they "retrodict"[61] the past, meaning that they attempt to infer what the past was like on the basis of the evidence at their disposal.

LAWS OF JEWISH HISTORY

Are there historical laws similar to scientific laws? Lord Acton's famous dictum, "All power corrupts, and absolute power corrupts absolutely," might be considered a historical law. W. H. Walsh referred to Lord Acton's apothegm as a historical lesson,[62] which does not have the necessary, binding, or causative connotation as does the concept "law."

If there are such phenomena as historical laws, they are to be discovered by induction. Through a large sample of similar experiences, one might be able to draw general conclusions concerning them. Since Jewish history extends from ancient days, covering a long time span, whether there are any laws operating within Jewish history might be a ripe area for speculation. One should beware, however, not to expect historical laws to be as firm as scientific ones because while historical events might be repeated in a similar manner, scientific data repeat in an identical fashion.

An example of an apparent law of Jewish history is this: The Sifrei asserts, "It is a known law that Essau hates Jacob."[63] This does not mean that there is enmity between every Jew and Gentile. Rather, in the flow of history anti-Semitism always seems to surface in one form or another. A second historical law is that the Jewish people are immortal, indestructible. The ancient Passover Haggada observed that "in every generation there are those who rise up against us to destroy us, and the Holy One Blessed Be He rescues us from their hand." This old dictum has held true, even in our own day. The holiday of Purim is celebrated by the Jewish people in the month of Adar. However, in the past there have been many special Purims celebrated by various Jewish communities to commemorate rescues of the Jewish people throughout history.[64] A third law of Jewish history is that the Torah will never be completely forgotten by the Jews.[65] Not only is the survival and continuous existence of the Jewish people a source for wonder, so is the survival of Torah learning and scholarship among the Jews. Considering the great suffering throughout the Jewish past, their scholarly achievements are a marvel. In the recent past, the United States was called a *treifa medina*, a land where traditional Judaism cannot flourish. Who would have thought that the study of Torah and religious life would blossom on arid American soil the way it has? Israel is the Holy Land, but the Jewish state originated along secular lines with a group of people who rarely showed much sympathy toward Jewish religious practice and studies. But the Torah of Israel would not be forgotten, and is studied avidly in the Land of Israel.

PATTERNS OF JEWISH HISTORY

Those who speculate about history often seek to find a pattern in history. Some, like Condorcet or Kant, believed that history follows a linear pattern, flowing in one direction, whether progressive or regressive. Most who hold this theory maintain that history follows a progressive pattern. Others, like Oswald Spengler, accept a cyclical pattern of history, with cycles repeating themselves among people and eras. Vico combined the linear and cyclical theories by positing that history advances spirally. Hegel taught that there is a linear development of human freedom in history, but saw a three-stage dialectical pattern in the histories of various peoples. Of course, there are many thinkers who believe that there is no pattern at all in human history.[66]

The next question, predictably, is whether there is a pattern or patterns within Jewish history? The recurrent themes of persecution, migration, and new beginnings run throughout Jewish history. The fall of the old and almost concurrent rise of new centers of Jewish settlement seem to occur as a rhythm from earliest times until our own days.

The rabbis of the Talmud and Midrash loved to find orderliness within historical events. Writing about the medieval historian and philosopher Rabbi Abraham Ibn Daud (1110–c. 1180), Professor Gerson D. Cohen (1924–1991) stated, "Parallelism and symmetry were second nature to a rabbinically trained mind, and Ibn Daud's collation of historical events was thus but a continuation of a well-established literary-theological scheme."[67] An example of this type of thinking is found in the Gemara: "When Rabbi Akiva died, Rabbi was born; when Rabbi died, Rav Yehudah was born; when Rav Yehudah died, Rava was born; when Rava died, Rav Ashi was born.[68] This teaches that a righteous man does not depart from the world until (another) righteous man like himself is created, as it is said, 'The sun riseth and the sun goeth down.'[69] Before Eli's sun was extinguished, the sun of Samuel of Ramoth rose."[70]

This search for patterns, symmetry, and orderliness within history satisfies the human need for familiarity and comfort. Professor Cohen wrote, "According to Ibn Daud, history not only legitimizes the past and the present; it also comforts and, by implication, gives hope for the future. History is a kind of sermon, a medium of insight into the workings of Providence and, accordingly, a vehicle of solace for Israel."[71] The concept of pattern implies design, order, neatness, symmetry, and harmony and thus introduces us to the aesthetics of history. Sometimes we not only want history to comfort, but also to please.

CLASSIFICATION AND JEWISH HISTORY

Another reason to search for historical patterns is to acquire a better understanding of history. The historian, though, tries to understand history not so much via a search for patterns and historical schemata but rather, like a scientist, utilizing the tool of classification, which in historical study usually means periodization. Examples of classification and periodization in general history are the dividing of the subject into ancient, medieval, and modern history; or into the history of the West and the East.

Classification for the historian implies that there are chunks or groups of events that have a certain similarity within themselves and a distinction from others. Therefore, they can be studied as separate units. Naturally, the division between different eras is not always clear-cut. Unlike geographical boundaries, there is no precise line of historical demarcation between medieval and modern history, for instance, and the division might be different for different peoples and nationalities. Nevertheless, despite the difficulties involved in determining criteria for classification and then fitting the details into a logical scheme, classification is used by historians as part of the historical method of understanding and interpreting the past.

Historical classification also preoccupied Jewish historians. Simon Dubnow divided Jewish history into the Oriental and the Occidental phases. The Oriental was subdivided into three parts: (1) the absolute Oriental period from the beginning of the appearance of the Hebrews until the fall of the Persian Empire (333 B.C.E.); (2) the Oriental-Occidental period from the beginning of the Hellenistic period (333 B.C.E.) until the destruction of the second Temple in 70 C.E.; (3) the period of the Palestinian and Babylonian centers from 70 C.E. until 1000. Dubnow also subdivided the Occidental phase of Jewish history into three periods: (1) the periods of Spanish, French, and German hegemony, from 1000 until 1500; (2) the period of German-Polish hegemony, from 1500 until 1789; (3) the modern period, from 1789 onward.[72]

The classification of Jewish history into various periods occupied historian Ben Zion Dinur a great deal. For instance, he dated the beginning of the Jewish Diaspora not with the destruction of the second Temple nor with the defeat after the Bar Kochva revolt in 135 C.E. Rather he believed that it commenced with the Arab conquest of Palestine in 637.[73] While Graetz affirmed that modern Jewish history started with the Haskala in 1750 and Dubnow thought that it began with the French Revolution in 1789, Dinur dated the beginning of modern Jewish history with the year 1700, when one thousand Jews led by Rabbi Judah the Pious immigrated to Palestine.[74]

It should be mentioned that the classification of ancient, medieval, and modern periods in general history do not coincide chronologically with those divisions in Jewish history. For instance, in European history, the conquest of Rome in 410 marks the end of ancient history and the beginning of the medieval period. The Renaissance is usually considered the end of the Middle Ages and the beginning of the modern period. In Jewish history, the medieval period is said to begin with the advent of Constantine the Great, the first Roman emperor who issued laws limiting the rights of Jewish citizens within the Roman Empire. The modern period of Jewish history, as mentioned, began not with the Renaissance but some time in the eighteenth century.

Besides chronological differences concerning the terms "ancient," "medieval," and "modern" between world and Jewish history, there is a variation in the content of these periods within these histories. A few examples illustrate this point. First, in ancient times the Jews lived in a theocratic state, where religion and government were intertwined. In general European history, such a situation existed in the medieval period rather than in the ancient one. In the Middle Ages, the masses of Europe were mainly illiterate. Literacy was reserved almost exclusively to the clergy, the educated class. Within medieval Jewry, literacy was widespread, not an exclusive privilege of the rabbis. The modern era of world history ushered in a period of progress, humanism, enlightenment, and tolerance, but for the Jews modernity also meant anti-Semitism, pogroms, extermination, and anti-Israel sentiments.

Classification is a tool for understanding history in toto, and also for comprehending specific eras and aspects of history. Professor Yehezkel Kaufmann, in his monumental history of the Biblical era, divided that era into five periods. First there is the age of the Patriarchs; followed by the time of Moses; which is succeeded by the age of the Judges; then the era of Kings Saul, David, and Solomon; and finally the fifth period includes the kings who lived after them.[75]

Professor Gedaliah Alon (1901–1950), in his *History of the Jews in Their Land in the Talmudic Age* divided that period of about six hundred years in Palestine into three divisions of time. Stage one is the Time of the Tannaim (70–235), stage two is the Age of the Amoraim (235–420), and stage three is Byzantine Palestine (420–640).[76] Alon recognized the problems involved in historical classification and periodization. He remarked that some of the boundaries posited by the historian are imaginary ones, and some events straddle boundaries or periods of classification. He asked what criteria should determine where one chapter ends and the next one begins? Should these criteria be political, socioeconomic, or cultural-intellectual? Changes in these major areas of human life do not always occur simultaneously. However, despite the problems, Alon believed that breaking historical time into chronological units has two purposes: bringing out the characteristics of each time segment and pointing out what is common to all time segments, thus indicating the flow of history.[77]

Meyer Waxman, in his five-volume *History of Jewish Literature*, encountered a different problem in historical classification. Should he present the entire subject matter in chronological form, or should he treat each branch of Jewish literature separately? Should he adopt a synchronic horizontal or a diachronic vertical approach? Waxman opted for the latter. Thus, to get an overview of the literary output of Rabbi Saadia Gaon (882–942) or of Maimonides, one will have to consult several chapters in Waxman's work because the literary activity of these two giants of Judaism falls into several genres of creativity.[78] In the *History of Jewish Literature* by Israel Zinberg, the horizontal approach is employed, and a figure like Rabbi Judah HaLevi (c. 1075–1141) or Maimonides is written about in a single chapter. There are advantages and disadvantages to each approach, which Waxman recognized.[79]

GOALS AND MEANING IN JEWISH HISTORY

Those who think about history frequently wonder whether there are goals within history (and for this inquiry, whether there are goals in Jewish history)? People have goals in their individual lives. They also act with purpose when they endeavor to offer better opportunities for their children, that they should live in a better society than their own. Thus people, the makers of history, operate with teleological orientation. In this sense, there are goals in history. There is an anecdote of the Emperor Hadrian asking a one-hundred-year-old man who was planting a tree whether he expected to eat from it? The old man replied, "If I am worthy, I shall eat; but if not, as my fathers labored for me, so I labor for my children." [80] People do live with goals for future generations, including Jews, as evidenced by the stress they put on education.

When considering the goal or goals of Jewish history, the idea of Messianism immediately comes to mind. Maimonides included the belief in the coming of the Messiah as one of his thirteen principles of Jewish faith. There are differences of opinion within Jewish sources about the nature of the Messianic age; but all agree that it is a utopian golden age of the future. Maimonides regarded the Messianic era as one of political deliverance of the Jews from non-Jewish rule, with no upheaval in the order of the world and with no apocalyptic elements. "In the days of the Messiah," he wrote, "in this world things will go on as usual, except that Israel will have its own government. . . . There would be no difference between the world of today and the days of the Messiah except for the obliteration of oppressive governments." [81]

Related to this subject of the goals of history is the question of whether history has meaning? The concept of "meaning" is ambiguous. What is the meaning of "meaning?" We are not concerned presently with "meaning" as definition, having already explained the definition of history as *meaning* the human past and its study. The question of the "meaning of history" in the present context refers to whether history has significance or importance, whether the concept of value can be attached to human history? For the Jewish mind, everything has meaning in the Divine and human scheme of things, including Jewish and world history.

The question of meaning and purpose has contemporary import in the thought centering around the Holocaust. Is there any purpose to the Holocaust? Why did it occur? Can there be meaning in such absurdity and horror? Can there be value in such cruelty? Did so many people suffer and lose their lives without there being some significance to what transpired? Why did God permit such horror to happen? Why did He not enter "deus ex machina" and stop the killings?

Some like Professor Richard Rubenstein (b. 1924) believe that it is impossible to accept the traditional concept of God after the Holocaust. Others, like Dr. Eliezer Berkovits (1908–1992), believe that God is not to blame for the events that transpired. Man did the killings, and he is the guilty one for misusing his freedom. Some maintain that the secularist, profane philosophy of western civilization with its materialistic, naturalistic outlook was the fault. Why blame God and religion for the failures of man and secularism? There are those who think that the Holocaust is unique in world history, whereas others think it is the same old story of Jewish persecution, magnified greatly by twentieth-century technology and German thoroughness. To Dr. Berkovits and to Professor Michael Wyshogrod (b. 1928), the theological problem is the same whether one Jew or six million are slaughtered.[82] Rabbi Yitzchok Hutner (1907–1980) did not accept the Holocaust as an isolated event in Jewish history. There had been previous destructions of the Jews, and he referred to the Holocaust as *Churban*, or destruction of European Jewry. The destruction of European Jewry is an integral part of the *Tocheicha*[83] (rebuke and punishment) phenomenon recorded in the Torah. Rabbi Hutner saw a pattern in Jewish history of destruction, exile, and redemption.[84]

Professor Emil Fackenheim (b. 1916) regarded the Holocaust as an "epoch-making" event in Jewish history. Its meaning for him involves a new imperative: "Jews are forbidden to hand Hitler posthumous victories." Therefore, the 614th commandment is that Jews must remain Jewish.[85]

The quest for meaning is not mere speculation or practiced only for philosophical indulgence. Rather it is an integral part of human living. The psychiatrist Viktor Frankl (1905–1997), himself a Holocaust survivor, wrote that "the striving to find a meaning in one's life is the primary motivational force in man."[86] He was fond of quoting Nietzsche: "He who has a 'why' to live can bear with almost any 'how.'"[87] This psychological and perhaps ontological need for meaning in life undoubtedly exists on a personal level. However, the urge to find meaning transfers to a longing to find meaning for society and for history as a whole.

CAUSATION AND JEWISH HISTORY

After dealing with these speculative and lofty aspects of Jewish history, we shall descend the ladder to the more mundane. The next problem to be dealt with is causation in history. We want to find out "why things happen" not in the teleological sense but in the natural, causative connotation. There are many factors that determine, or at least influence, the course of history. Some theorists single out one factor as the sole determinant force on history, or at least the predominant one. It appears more likely that there are many causes operating in history, some playing a more important role than others, depending upon the situation. We shall note some that function within Jewish history.

Montesquieu maintained that the differences in national character and culture are the result of differences in climate and geography.[88] There is no doubt that the geographical factor had a great influence on Jewish history. The fact that the Land of Israel is situated geographically between Egypt and what used to be the Babylonian, Assyrian, and—later—Seleucid empires converted it into a battleground on which, and over which, countless military battles were fought. In the Bible, we read about alliances, intrigues, wars, and revolts between the Israelites and their neighbors.

Karl Marx (1818–1883) taught that history is determined entirely by economics. Economics, of course, also played a significant role in Jewish history. In the Middle Ages, for instance, Jews were denied agricultural opportunities for making a living and were barred from joining the guilds. Consequently many became interest-charging moneylenders. This occupation, naturally, did not lead to the enhancement of their popularity, and Jews have frequently been maligned and caricatured as usurers.

In Poland, many Jews were managers of the estates of Polish noblemen, with the entailing obligation of collecting rent and taxes from the peasants. For this, again, they did not win a prize for popularity, and they became targets for massacre during the Chmelniecki pogroms in 1648–1649. In our own day, some attribute anti-Semitism among Blacks partially to the economic superiority of Jewish businessmen and landlords, whom Blacks accuse of exploiting them economically.

If any one factor is the paramount causative agent within Jewish history, it is religion. Religion, as would be expected, plays an essential role in events throughout Jewish history. The Maccabean wars, for example, were fought because of religious reasons. The Jews were exiled from Spain when they refused to renounce their religion. Much of the literary and scholarly activity of the Jews throughout the past and in the present is of a religious nature. Religious law is an important ingredient in the legal system of the State of Israel, and religious parties play a significant role within the Israeli government.

History, quite obviously, was made by people. Emerson told us that "There is properly no history, only biography." Carlyle similarly wrote, "Biography is the only true history."[89] Collingwood, in a more philosophical vein, believed that it is not sufficient for the historian to discover mere events, he has to know the ideas expressed in them. Since the "historical process is a process of thought," it is obvious why history limits its knowledge to human affairs.[90]

It would be possible to write history in biographical terms, if one were to stretch the usual meaning of biography. One could write the history of the Hebrews from their origins through the time of the Prophet Samuel by writing an unusually thorough biography of Moses. One could begin this biography by describing pre-Mosaic times as an introduction to his life, delineating the formation of individual Jewish families from the times of the Patriarchs until they entered Egypt. Then one could continue with a description of life in Egypt, Moses' role in Egyptian Jewish life and in his bringing about the Exodus, his role at Sinai and in the desert, how his work was continued through Joshua's entering the Land of Israel, and the tribal existence of the people during the period of the Judges until the appearance of Samuel. A second phase of Jewish history could center around a very thorough biography of King David, which would describe pre-Davidic times from Samuel and King Saul, proceed with the events of David's life and times, and conclude with how the Davidic kingdom fared until its division in the time of his grandson, Reheboam. It is conceivable that a coherent, complete history of the Jewish people could be composed around the lives of some of its seminal figures throughout the ages. The advantage of this unusual approach to historical writing is that it is often more interesting to read about the lives of influential people than about historical processes.

A philosophical issue regarding the connection between history and biography is whether and to what extent men determine the course of history, or are their actions determined by the conditions or *zeitgeist* of the times in which they live? Is man the master of his historical destiny, or merely the one who acts it out?

Professor Sidney Hook (1902–1989) distinguished between the *eventful* man and the *event-making* man. The eventful man is compared to the little Dutch boy who kept his finger in the hole in the dike and thereby rescued the town. What he did had tremendous significance for the community, but anyone with lots of patience could have done it. The event-making man is an eventful man whose actions are the consequences of outstanding capacities of intelligence, will, and character rather than of accidents of position.[91]

Regarding the event-making man, it can be asked if his accomplishments are *sui generis*, or whether they would have been repeated or simulated by another great man, another hero or villain in history, had he not lived?

Rabbi Yochanan ben Zakkai is regarded as a pivotal figure during the time of the destruction of the Second Temple in 70 C.E. It is related that when he became convinced of the Roman victory and of the coming of the great national tragedy, he requested of Vespasian, the Roman general and emperor-to-be, that he be granted the town of Jamnia (Yavneh) and its wise men.[92] With this act, he was able to set up a nucleus of Torah study and to maintain some of the institutions that had been connected with the Holy Sanctuary in Jerusalem, thus providing the foundation for the continuous existence of the Jewish people in a time of terrible crisis. There is no question that Rabbi Yochanan ben Zakkai had great foresight and was an outstanding, courageous leader. The question arises: what would have happened if Rabbi Yochanan ben Zakkai had not been alive at this critical time? Would someone else have acted so wisely in his place? If so, or if not, how would things have turned out differently for the Jewish people both then and now?

This issue of the role of heroes in history is related to the question of "What would have happened if" slightly different things had occurred in many junctures of general or Jewish history? Sometimes the history of the world depends on major events or personalities and sometimes on trivial details. Concerning the latter, Pascal commented, "Cleopatra's nose, had it been shorter, the whole aspect of world history would have been different."[93] An example of such "what if" speculation regarding the history of Rabbinic literature is the following: What would have happened if Maimonides had cited the sources for his legal decisions in the *Mishneh Torah* code? It is doubtful that the *Baal Hasagot* would have gone out of business, but perhaps Jewish legal literature would have developed differently. The "what if" inquiry concerning this question and others is interesting, if merely theoretical.

Two instances from modern Jewish history come to mind regarding the "what if" and the relationship and interaction of the hero or villain with the zeitgeist. What if Hitler had not existed? Would there have been another villain like him, causing the same or a similar Holocaust? Was the appearance of such a scoundrel an inevitability considering the rampant anti-Semitism and the historical, ideological background of post-World War I Germany? Or was the individual Hitler just a terribly bad break for his victims and for all mankind? Perhaps, had he not lived, those terrible events would not have happened?

The other example is Theodore Herzl (1860–1904). If Herzl had not written *The Jewish State*, conducted his international Zionist political activities, and convened the World Zionist Congresses, would the State of Israel have been proclaimed in 1948? If there were no Russian pogroms in the 1880s, no Dreyfus Affair in 1894—thus no early Zionist activity—would the State of Israel have been established when it was, even considering the post-Holocaust guilt feelings of the countries of the world?

BIBLICAL VIEW OF HISTORY

Collingwood wrote that in Hegel's work "history for the first time steps out full grown on the stage of philosophical thought."[94] Thinkers like Vico, Hegel, Spengler, and Toynbee were among the great systematizers of world history. Rabbi Nachman Krochmal presented us with a grandiose philosophy of Jewish history, and there is a theory of Jewish and world history contained in the Bible, though it is not enunciated explicitly and systematically in the latter. We shall conclude this chapter with an exposition of the Biblical philosophy of history, to be followed by Krochmal's.

The philosophy of history begins with the Hebrew Bible. Hermann Cohen (1842–1918) affirmed that "the concept of history is the product of prophetism."[95] Nicolas Berdyaev wrote, "An authentic conception of history was foreign to Hellenic consciousness. Its origin must be sought rather in the consciousness and spirit of ancient Israel. It was the Jews who contributed the concept of 'historical' to world history."[96]

The awareness of history was also alien to the Eastern mind. Hindus, for example, are committed to an extreme form of spiritualism, the whole earthly scheme being *maya*, or illusion. Temporal history thus becomes devoid of meaning.[97] A historical sensibility could not be cultivated with this kind of world view.

The ancient Greeks also had a strong antihistorical tendency in their thought. According to them, anything that can be an object of genuine knowledge must be of a permanent nature. Mathematics is such a knowledge par excellence. History deals more with the transient than with the permanent, and could not be considered by the Greeks of primary importance.[98]

Plato devalued the empirical and mutable, and believed that true reality rests in the timeless world of ideas.[99] Aristotle brushed aside the particular and individual as merely accidental phenomena or occurrences.[100] He wrote, "Poetry is something more philosophic and of greater import than history, since its statements are of the nature of universals, whereas those of history are singular."[101] The Stoics spoke of the great cosmic fire in which the entire universe was periodically consumed, only to begin again anew. "And so there will be another Socrates and another Athenian jury that will again sentence him to death."[102] According to this doctrine of eternal recurrence, only the timeless and eternal retain any value.[103] The Greeks had no view of the world and history, even though there is Greek historiography.[104] For the first positive and fruitful interpretation of history, one has to turn to the books of the Hebrew Bible.

Professor Abraham Joshua Heschel (1907–1972) wrote, "Judaism is a religion of history, a religion of time."[105] The importance of history within the Bible is well illustrated by the wording of the first of the Ten

Commandments, "I the Lord am your God who brought you out of the land of Egypt, the house of bondage."[106] It is not written "your God who created the cosmos"—rather a historical category is employed.

The Bible views history as occurring between two states of felicity. At the beginning, there was the creation of the world and the placing of man in paradise, or the Garden of Eden. At the end of days comes the Messianic era, or redemption. In between these two periods occur the happenings known as history.[107]

The Bible portrays history as progressing in a linear direction, though not in a straight line, and sees the actions of men as progressive, though intermittently so, leading finally to the hoped-for end, the redemption. History does not move in endless circles. "It gets somewhere, it accomplishes something, it has meaning to God and man alike."[108]

The idea of history having a Messianic goal is beautifully expressed in the book of Isaiah in the following two passages:

> In the days to come,
> The Mount of the Lord's House
> Shall stand firm above the mountains
> And tower above the hills;
> And all the nations
> Shall gaze on it with joy.
> And the many peoples shall go and say:
> 'Come,
> Let us go up to the Mount of the Lord,
> To the House of the God of Jacob;
> That He may instruct us in His ways,
> And that we may walk in His paths.'
> For instruction shall come forth from Zion
> The word of the Lord from Jerusalem.
> Thus He will judge among the nations
> And arbitrate for the many peoples,
> And they shall beat their swords into plowshares
> And their spears into pruning hooks:

Nation shall not take up
Sword against nation;
They shall never again know war." [109]

"But a shoot shall grow out of the stump of Jesse,
A twig shall sprout from his stock.
The spirit of the Lord shall alight upon him:
A spirit of wisdom and insight,
A spirit of counsel and valor,
A spirit of devotion and reverence for the Lord.
He shall sense the truth by his reverence for the Lord:
He shall not judge by what his eyes behold,
Nor decide by what his ears perceive.
Thus he shall judge the poor with equity
And decide with justice for the lowly of the land.
He shall strike down a land with the rod of his mouth
And slay the wicked with the breath of his lips.
Justice shall be the girdle of his loins,
And faithfulness the girdle of his waist.
The wolf shall dwell with the lamb,
The leopard lie down with the kid;
The calf, the beast of prey, and the fatling together,
With a little boy to herd them.
The cow and the bear shall graze,
Their young shall lie down together;
And the lion, like the ox, shall eat straw.
A babe shall play
Over a viper's hole,
And an infant pass his hand
Over an adder's den.
In all of My sacred mount
Nothing evil or vile shall be done;
For the land shall be filled with devotion to the Lord
As water covers the sea." [110]

The Bible pictures history as having a goal, and the events transpiring therein as having a meaning. Karl Loewth asserted that this eschatological outlook toward the future fulfilment of history is the source and origin of the modern historical consciousness.[111]

The Biblical conception of history is forward-looking, meaningful, teleological, and has a happy ending. How, on the other hand, does the Bible account for the process of history? How does it explain historical occurrences? What is the role of God in history? Is the historical pattern predetermined by God? What role do the mighty national powers and empires play in history? There are two pertinent passages in the Bible that answer these questions:

> And the Israelites did what was offensive to the Lord. They worshiped the Baalim and forsook the Lord, the God of their fathers, who had brought them out of the Land of Egypt. They followed other gods, from among the gods of the peoples around them, and bowed down to them; they provoked the Lord. . . . Then the Lord was incensed at Israel, and He handed them over to foes who plundered them. He surrendered them to their enemies on all sides, and they could no longer hold their own against their enemies. . . . Then the Lord raised up chieftains who delivered them from those who plundered them. But they did not heed their chieftains either; they went astray after other gods and bowed down to them. They were quick to turn aside from the way their fathers had followed in obedience to the commandments of the Lord; they did not do right. . . .[112]
>
> Ha!
>
> Assyria, rod of my anger,
> In whose hand, as a staff, is my fury!
> I send him against an ungodly nation,
> I charge him against a people that provokes Me,
> To take its spoil and to seize its booty

And to make it a thing trampled
Like the mire of the streets.
But he has evil plans,
His mind harbors evil designs;
For he means to destroy,
To wipe out nations, not a few.[113]

The historical process as described in Scripture is a "Divine-human encounter in which God calls to man, man in his pride defies God, and God in His judgment punishes sinful man."[114] The essence of Hebraism is contingent upon the historical. The very inception of the Hebrews as a people took place at a moment in time, at the foot of Mount Sinai. It was then that the Israelites entered a covenant with the Deity. Israel agreed to observe the Divine Torah, and for keeping their side of the agreement, God will watch over them and preserve their well-being.[115]

If the Israelites do not live up to the terms of the Divine Covenant and deviate from the ways commanded by the Lord, they are punished for their disobedience. How are they punished? God sends mighty nations against Israel, nations that are instruments of judgment in the hand of the Lord.[116] These foreign peoples, whether they be Israel's immediate neighbors or the mighty powers of Assyria and Babylonia, were the means utilized by God for retribution against the recalcitrant Hebrews. Jewish history appears as an arena for carrying out Divine justice as the Israelites relate to the Covenant.

History according to the Bible is, to paraphrase Hegel, the march of God and man in history. Originally man was in a paradisal state of perfection, with political history and international relations resulting from the sins of man. As Karl Loewth put it, "Without original sin and final redemption the historical interim would be unnecessary and unintelligible."[117]

Just as the Hebrews believed in God, the Creator of heaven and earth, they also affirmed that He is the Lord of the entire historical process, and is concerned about all the peoples who inhabit the earth. Did not Jonah prophesy to Nineveh? Amos and Isaiah directed some of their prophecies to other nations besides their own.[118] Amos wrote these incisive words about the relationship of Israel with the other nations:

> To Me, O Israelites, you are
> Just like the Ethiopians—Declares the Lord.
> True, I brought Israel up
> From the land of Egypt,
> But also the Philistines from Caphtor
> And the Arameans from Kir.[119]

History is conceived as the realization of the word of God.[120] However, the word of God is influenced by the deeds of men. If men obey God and are moral, times are auspicious; if they do not, there is havoc on the national and international scenes. Not only is Israel subject to retribution for disobeying God, the other nations are also judged on the basis of their conduct. In the first two chapters of the Book of Amos, we see that other peoples are punished for the moral atrocities they have committed. About one nation, for instance, he wrote:

> Thus said the Lord:
> For three transgressions of the Ammonites,
> For four, I will not revoke it:
> Because they ripped open the pregnant women of Gilead
> In order to enlarge their own territory.
> I will set fire to the wall of Rabbah,
> And it shall devour its fortresses,
> Amid shouting on a day of battle,
> On a day of violent tempest.
> Their king and his officers shall go
> Into exile together—said the Lord.[121]

The Bible contains not only historiosophy, but also historiography. It constitutes not only a system of laws and norms, but has also within its pages a record of historical happenings.[122] Historical narrative is found in the Pentateuch, the prophets, Esther, Daniel, Ezra, Nehemiah, and Chronicles. To understand the nature of Biblical historiography, one has to keep in mind that the historical writings of the Bible are a product of its philosophy of history.[123] Maintaining a view of history that centers around the Divine, as well as the human, leads to a writing of history with theological underpinnings.

KROCHMAL'S PHILOSOPHY OF JEWISH HISTORY

Another major philosophical treatment of Jewish history is to be found in the *Moreh Nevuchei HaZeman*, the "Modern Guide for the Perplexed," authored by Rabbi Nachman Krochmal. Krochmal was the first modern Jewish philosopher who made the Jewish people, not simply Judaism, the subject of philosophical investigation. He not only described the course of Jewish history, but interpreted it in a philosophical-historical manner.[124] His interest in philosophy and history were subservient to the central preoccupation of his life, which was the understanding of Judaism in its historical manifestation.[125] He was greatly influenced by German idealistic philosophy, particularly by Schelling, whose metaphysical conception of God as the Absolute he accepted and clothed in Hegelian terminology.[126]

Krochmal, like Vico and Herder, affirmed that every nation is an integrated whole that has its own form of spirituality and creates its own heritage.[127] A nation is a spiritual organism, and therefore passes through the life cycle of growth, maturity, and decline. Decline for a civilization occurs as a result of the desire for luxury and power.[128] Krochmal accepted a progressive, linear pattern of history, for he maintained that after the demise of a nation, other nations take over and develop its outstanding traits. For example, the accomplishments of Greece were absorbed by Rome.[129]

There is, nevertheless, a *people* who is eternal. From the beginning of its national existence, only Israel had faith in the Absolute Spirit, becoming the teacher of mankind. This adherence to the Absolute Spirit exempted the Jewish people from the destruction that is the fate of all other people. However, since the Jewish nation is a social organism, the triadic historical law that all nations grow, mature, and decay also applies to Israel. But just as Israel is about to degenerate, its spiritual power is renewed, and it enters another three-stage cycle. Because Judaism is rooted in the eternal Absolute, Israel regenerates itself after periods of decline and does not disappear from the arena of history.[130]

Krochmal has divided all of Jewish history into four triadic cycles: (1) from the Patriarchs until the Babylonian exile, with the period of maturity from Israel's settlement in Canaan until the death of King Solomon; (2) from the Babylonian exile until the Bar Kochva revolt in 135 C.E., with the maturity period being from Alexander the Great's death until the death of Queen Salome Alexandra in 67 B.C.E.; (3) from 135 C.E. until the seventeenth century; and (4) from the seventeenth century onward.[131]

R. Nachman Krochmal's *Moreh Nevuchei HaZeman* was published posthumously. It was the first modern exposition of a philosophy of Jewish history, and is probably still the most profound.

ENDNOTES

1. Joseph L. Baron, *A Treasury of Jewish Quotations* (New York: Crown Publishers, 1956), p. 181, note 383. B.

2. Sota 47a. See also T. J. Yoma, ch. 4, near beginning.

3. See Dubnow's introduction to his *World History of the Jewish People*. This spaciotemporal quality calls for a relativity-like theory in order to comprehend Jewish history. For instance, if one wants to understand the events of a particular chronological era, he or she must simultaneously refer to a specific geographical area because the events of Jewish history differ from place to place, even during the same period of time. Thus time and space are not absolute, but are interrelated.

4. A refutation of Toynbee's views regarding Jewish history is found in Maurice Samuel, *The Professor and the Fossil* (New York: Alfred A. Knopf, 1956).

5. Hans Meyerhoff, ed., *The Philosophy of History in Our Time* (New York: Doubleday Anchor, 1969), p. 25.

6. William H. Dray, "Philosophy of History", in *The Encyclopedia of Philosophy*, op. cit., vol. 6, p. 251.

7. William H. Dray, *Philosophy of History* (Englewood Cliffs, N.J.: Prentice-Hall, 1964), p. 60.

8. W. H. Walsh, *An Introduction to Philosophy of History* (London: Hutchinson's University Press, 1953), p. 156.

9. Dray, op. cit., in *The Encyclopedia of Philosophy*, op. cit., p. 247.

10. Walsh, op. cit., p. 15.

11. Ibid., p. 14.

12. Raymond Aron, "Relativism in History," in Meyerhoff, op. cit., pp. 155–156.

13. Avot 2:1.

14. Yosef Hayim Yerushalmi, *Zakhor* (Philadelphia: Jewish Publication Society, 1982), p. 102, where Jorge Luis Borges's story, "Funes et memorioso," reveals what it is like to forget nothing.

15. The "scissors and paste" phrase was used by R. G. Collingwood in his *The Idea of History* (New York: Galaxy Books, 1956), p. 33, 36, 125–26, 143, 257–66, 269–70, 274–81, 319.

16. Achad-HaAm (1856–1927) made the distinction between archaeological truth, the way things actually occurred, and historical truth, the way they are remembered. Martin Buber referred to the former as history and the latter as saga. See Martin Buber, "Biblical Leadership" in Martin Buber, *On the Bible*, ed. by Nahum N. Glatzer, (New York: Schocken Books, 1982), p. 137.

17. Fritz Stern, *The Varieties of History* (New York: Meridian Books 1956), pp. 54–57. Ranke aspired to record history *wie es eigentlich gewesen.*

18. Evan Esar, *Dictionary of Humorous Quotations* (New York: Paperback Library, 1962), p. 44.

19. R. G. Collingwood compared the historian's task to that of a detective's. See his *The Idea of History*, op cit., pp. 243, 266–268, etc.

20. Benedetto Croce, *History: Its Theory and Practice*, excerpts in Meyerhoff, op. cit., pp. 45–46.

21. Meyerhoff, op. cit., p. 44.

22. Augustin Thierry, "Letters on the History of France.," in Stern, op. cit., p. 64.

23. The secular, political, and military historical writings that are cited in the Bible have not survived. They include "Chronicles of the Kings of Judah" and "Chronicles of the Kings of Israel," mentioned in the Book of Kings.

24. Such works include Meiri's "Introduction to Avot," Ibn Daud's *Book of Tradition*, Zacuto's *Book of Genealogy*, Halperin's *Seder HaDorot*, etc.

25. Such works include Ibn Verga's *Shevet Yehuda* and Joseph HaCohen's *Emek HaBacha.*

26. Croce, op. cit., in Meyerhoff, op. cit., p. 51.

27. Meyer Waxman, *A History of Jewish Literature*, vol. III., (New York: Bloch, 1945), pp. 541–542.

28. Yerushalmi, op. cit., p. 132, note 31. Professor Yerushalmi wrote that this view of Jewish history as one of martyrology and listing the "chain of tradition" might constitute "the one line of continuity between Wissenschaft and the Middle Ages."

29. Cecil Roth, "Historiography," in *Encyclopedia Judaica*, (Jerusalem: Keter Publishing House, 1972), vol. 8, p. 561.

30. Waxman, op. cit., p. 538.

31. Ibid., p. 541.

32. Roth, op. cit., p. 561.

33. Gotthard Deutsch, "Graetz, Heinrich," in *The Jewish Encyclopedia*, Reprint of *The Jewish Encyclopedia*, (New York: Funk & Wgnalls, 1901–1905) (New York: Ktav [No Date]), vol. 6, p. 67.

34. Shmuel Ettinger, article on "Graetz, Heinrich" in *Encyclopedia Judaica*, vol. 7, p. 849.

35. Waxman, op. cit., vol. IV., pp. 735–748.

36. Haim Hillel Ben-Sasson, "Dubnow, Simon," in *Encyclopedia Judaica*, vol. 6, pp. 252–255.

37. Does the fact that Professor Baron resided in optimistic America have anything to do with his rejecting the "lachrymose" view of Jewish history?

38. Arthur Hertzberg, "Baron, Salo Wittmayer," in *Encyclopedia Judaica*, vol. 4, p. 254.

39. Yerushalmi, op. cit., p. 101.

40. Robert Alter, *Modern Hebrew Literature* (New York: Behrman House, 1975), p. 270.

41. Ibid., p. 268.

42. Walsh, op. cit., pp. 19–22, 94–118.

43. Ibid., p. 108.

44. Meyerhoff, op. cit., p. 188.

45. Stern, op. cit., p. 256.

46. The chapter on Jewish Education.

47. Yerushalmi, op. cit., pp. 32–33, 114–115.

48. Stern, op. cit., p. 31.

49. Terence Penelhum, "Personal Identity," in *Encyclopedia of Philosophy*, op. cit., vol. 6, pp. 95–107.

50. Nietzsche's views on history are found in his "Of the Use and Disadvantage of History for Life."

51. Henry Wadsworth Longfellow, "A Psalm of Life."

52. Esar, op. cit., p. 81.

53. Ibid., p. 160.

54. Ibid., p. 156.

55. Lev. 26:3–43, Deut. 27:15–28:68.

56. Judges 2:11–23, 3:5–15, 4:1–7, etc.

57. Amos 2:6. See Yehezkel Kaufmann, *The Religion of Israel* (Chicago: University of Chicago Press, 1960), pp. 365–366.

58. Haim Gevaryahu, "Kaufmann, Yehezkel," in *Encyclopedia Judaica*, vol. 16, p. 1351.

59. John B. Bury, "The Science of History," in Stern, op. cit., p. 210.

60. Thomas Buckle, "General Introduction to the History of Civilization in England," in Stern, op. cit., pp. 120–128.

61. W. H. Walsh believed that Professor Gilbert Ryle suggested the term "retrodict." See Walsh, op. cit., p. 41.

62. Ibid., p. 38.

63. Sifrei, Bihaalotecha, 69.

64. *Encyclopedia Judaica*, vol. 13, pp. 1395–1400. See also Philip Goodman, *The Purim Anthology* (Philadelphia: Jewish Publication Society, 1964), pp. 14–38.

65. See Rashi on Deut. 31:21.

66. William H. Dray, in *Encyclopedia of Philosophy*, op. cit., pp. 251–252, and Dray's *Philosophy of History*, op. cit., pp. 61–63.

67. Gerson D. Cohen, *The Book of Tradition* (Philadelphia: Jewish Publication Society, 1967), pp. 191–192.

68. In these mentioned instances, it appears that the respective births and deaths occurred on the same day.

69. Eccl. 1:5.

70. Kid. 72b and Yoma 38b. The saying, "The deeds of the Patriarchs are omens of what will transpire to their offspring" (Ramban's commentary to Lech Lecha 12:6) is another example of the search for historical patterns and symmetry.

71. Cohen, op. cit., pp. 190–191.

72. Simon Dubnow, *History of the Jews*, vol. 1, (New York: Thomas Yoseloff, 1967), pp. 33–38. See also Waxman, op. cit., vol. 4, p. 739.

73. Ben Zion Dinur, *Israel and the Diaspora* (Philadelphia: Jewish Publication Society, 1969), p. 3.

74. Ibid., p. 68. Professor Jonathan I. Israel of London asserted that modern Jewish history actually emerges from 1550 onward, when Jews were readmitted to countries west of Poland. He opposed the views of conventional historians who regard the sixteenth and seventeenth centuries as extensions of the Middle Ages for Jews. See George Wolf's review of Professor Israel's book, *European Jewry in the Age of Mercantilism, 1550–1750* (Oxford: Clarendon Press, 1985), in *Judaica Book News*, vol. 16, no. 2 (Spring/Summer 1986). It also should be noted that the dates given for the onset of modern Jewish history by the historians cited in our text are determined by their general outlook and understanding of Jewish history. Graetz, who stressed intellectual history, gave the Haskala central importance; Dunbow, who advocated social history, accepted the French Revolution as the turning point; and Dinur, who advocated a Land of Israel centered history, chose the date when one thousand Jews made *aliyah*, or settled in the Holy Land.

75. Yehezkel Kaufmann, *Toldot HaEmuna HaYisraelit*, vol. II, book 1, (Jerusalem: Mosad Bialik, 1957), introduction.

76. Gedaliah Alon, *The History of The Jews in Their Land in the Talmudic Age*, English edition, (Jerusalem: Magnes Press, 1980), pp. 20–38. Alon believed that the entire history of the Jewish people can be divided logically into two periods: the time before and the time since Christianity.

77. Ibid., pp. 18–21.

78. Waxman, op. cit., vol. I, preface.

79. Ibid.

80. Lev. R., XXXV., 5.

81. Maimonides, *Mishneh Torah*, Laws of Repentance, ch. 9.

82. Steven T. Katz, *Jewish Philosophers* (New York: Bloch, 1975), pp. 222–243.

83. Sections from the Torah portions of BeChukotai, Ki Tavo, and Nitzavim-VaYelech.

84. Rabbi Yitzchok Hutner, "Holocaust," in Nisson Wolpin ed., *A Path Through Fire* (Brooklyn, New York: Mesorah, 1986), pp. 39–55. This volume contains reflections on the Holocaust by Orthodox Jewish thinkers.

85. Katz, op. cit., pp. 228–233.

86. Viktor E. Frankl, *Man's Search for Meaning* (New York: Pocket Books, 1971), p. 154.

87. Gordon W. Allport, preface to Frankl, op. cit., p. xi.

88. Collingwood, op. cit., pp. 78–79.

89. Lewis C. Henry, *Best Quotations for All Occasions* (New York: Premier Books, 1945), pp. 21, 106.

90. Collingwood, op. cit., pp. 78–79.

91. Sidney Hook, *The Hero In History* (Boston: Beacon Press, 1955), p. 154.

92. Git. 56b.

93. Blaise Pascal, *Pensees*, quoted in Hook, op. cit., p. 176.

94. Collingwood, op. cit., p. 113.

95. Quoted in Will Herberg, *Judaism and Modern Man* (New York: Meridian, 1951), p. 209.

96. Nicolas Berdyaev, *Meaning of History* (London: Geoffrey Bles, 1936), p. 28.

97. Herberg, op. cit., p. 193.

98. Collingwood, op. cit., pp. 20–21.

99. Herberg, op. cit., p. 195.

100. Ibid.

101. Aristotle, *Poetics*, 1451:5–7.

102. Herberg, op. cit., p. 194.

103. Ibid.

104. Paul Tillich, *The Interpretation of History*, quoted by Herberg, op. cit., p. 209.

105. Abraham J. Heschel, *God in Search of Man* (Philadelphia: Jewish Publication Society, 1956), p. 200.

106. Exodus 20:2.

107. Herberg, op. cit., p. 211.

108. Ibid., p. 196.

109. Isaiah 2:2–4.

110. Isaiah 11:1–9.

111. Karl Loewth, *Meaning in History* (Chicago: University of Chicago Press, Phoenix Books, 1949), p. 196.

112. Judges 2:11–23.

113. Isaiah 10:5–7.

114. Herberg, op. cit., p. 219.

115. Julius Guttmann, *The Philosophy of Judaism* (English translation by David W. Silverman, New York: Holt, Rinehart and Winston, 1964), p. 11.

116. Ibid.

117. Loewth, op. cit., p. 184.

118. Amos 1:3–2:3, Isaiah, chapters 13–23.

119. Amos 9:7.

120. Yehezkel Kaufmann, *The History of the Hebrew Religion*, Hebrew Edition, Book IV, (Jerusalem and Tel Aviv: Mosad Bialik-Dvir, 1947), pp. 153–154.

121. Amos 1:13–15.

122. Heschel, op. cit., p. 200.

123. Kaufmann, op. cit., p. 154.

124. Guttmann, op. cit., pp. 322, 338.

125. Moshe Schwarcz, "Krochmal, Nachman," in *Encyclopedia Judaica*, vol. 10, p. 1270.

126. Guttmann, op. cit., p. 446, notes 37 and 54.

127. Robert M. Seltzer, *Jewish People, Jewish Thought* (New York: Macmillan, 1980), p. 576.

128. Will Durant noted that a civilization (or a nation?) is born Stoic and dies Epicurean.

129. Seltzer, op. cit., p. 576.

130. Guttmann, op. cit., pp. 338–339.

131. Ibid., pp. 339–340, and Seltzer, op. cit., pp. 576–578. For a Kabbalistic view of history and the Jewish role in it according to the Lurianic School, see Gershom G. Scholem, *Major Trends in Jewish Mysticism* (New York: Schocken, 1954), pp. 273–274, and his *Shabbatai Sevi: The Mystical Messiah* (Princeton, NJ: Princeton University Press, 1973), pp. 44–50. According to Lurianism, history forms the requisite background for the restoration (*tikkun*) of the original order that existed prior to the "breaking of the vessels" during the creation process. This *tikkun* is achieved by Israel performing the commandments with the proper intentions (*kavanot*), usually mystical, thereby liberating the holy sparks that became scattered among the nations and reuniting them. The attainment of this restoration will usher in the arrival of the Messiah.

THREE

Jewish Ethics

T here are many people who are turned off by philosophy because of its impracticality, its speculative and sometimes ethereal nature. Utilizing William James's phrase, philosophy rarely has cash value. Ethics, however, is a branch of philosophy with its roots planted in the ground. Aristotle referred to it as practical knowledge.[1] All of us favor ethics, and would like our neighbors to be ethical while recognizing our own ethical shortcomings. Even rogues have a code of ethics among themselves, for without it, their way of life would be even more problematic. The saying goes that when thieves fight, the peasant keeps his cow.[2] Without at least a semblance of ethical behavior, a human relationship—whether personal, group, or societal—undoubtedly would deteriorate and probably disintegrate. This is not to imply that ethics has only negative, survival value, that it is needed only to prevent decline. Although it serves that purpose also, in a positive vein ethical behavior leads to a good life both on an individual and on a collective level.

ETHICS IS FUNDAMENTAL TO JUDAISM

Ethics, of course, is fundamental to the Jewish religion. In the first book of the Bible we find the Patriarch Abraham taking God to task about whether He would destroy the wicked city of Sodom if it contained ten righteous inhabitants. "Will You sweep away the innocent along with the guilty?... Far be it from You to do such a thing, to bring death upon the innocent as well as the guilty, so that innocent and guilty fare alike. Far be it from You! Shall not the Judge of all the earth deal justly?"[3] It should be kept in mind that Abraham pleaded for the Sodomites, an early indication that Jewish ethics is not parochial but, rather, universal. The books of Exodus and Deuteronomy contain the ethical teaching of the Ten Commandments. In the latter book is found the lofty passage, "Justice, justice shall you pursue."[4] The verse named by Rabbi Akiva as the comprehensive principle of Torah is located in Leviticus: "Love your fellow as yourself."[5] The prophets are lauded as ethical teachers par excellence, frequently stressing the ethical over the ceremonial, or at least the *sine qua non* quality of the former as regards the efficacy of the latter.[6] Two verses from prophetic literature will be cited as illustrative of its lofty moral tone. In the book of Isaiah appears the verse:

I will restore your magistrates as of old,
And your counselors as of yore,
After that you shall be called
City of Righteousness, Faithful City.
Zion shall be saved by justice,
Her repentant ones by righteousness.[7]

Hosea relates the espousal of Israel to God in the following words:

And I will espouse you forever:
I will espouse you with righteousness and justice,
And with goodness and mercy,
And I will espouse you with faithfulness:
Then You shall be devoted to the Lord.[8]

The sublime book of Job, in the Hagiographic section of the Bible, wrestles with the ethical problem of theodicy, of the coexistence of God with injustice and suffering, undoubtedly the most difficult and troubling subject facing a thinking religious person.

The Talmud and Midrashim are also replete with portions concerning proper ethical conduct and principles. For example, the entire Mishnaic treatise *Avot*, which is also located in the Prayer book, is devoted to ethical matters.[9] Recent Jewish philosophy has been characterized by the preeminence it gives to the ethical aspect of Judaism. Professor Nathan Rotenstreich, writing about modern Jewish thought, stated, "What strikes us as new is the insistence on the primacy of ethics in the sphere of faith."[10]

The following recent incident is of interest regarding our topic. It is customary in *yeshivot* for young students to commence their Talmudic studies with the tractate *Bava Metzia* and continue the following year with *Bava Kamma* (tractates dealing with Jewish civil law). It was suggested to the renowned halachic authority Rabbi Moshe Feinstein (1895–1986) that students should start their Talmudic study with subject matter that is more relevant to their lives, such as *Pesachim* or *Berachot*. He remarked that beginning one's studies with *Bava Metzia* and *Bava Kamma* is an indication that Judaism does not start in the *Bet HaMidrash* (study hall and/or synagogue), but rather in the street. Judaism does not only mean praying, but also returning a lost item. Being religious means dealing with our fellow human beings in a proper fashion.[11] Obviously, Rabbi Feinstein did not equate Judaism with ethics nor did he relegate the remainder of the Halacha to the background. However, he pointed out the importance of ethics as a primary component of Judaism.

It is not always clear what is meant by the word "ethics." William Frankena wrote that there are three kinds of ethical inquiry. The first is descriptive and is the domain of anthropology, history, or sociology, and not of philosophy. The second is normative and deals with the *ought* as opposed to the *is* of descriptive ethics. Normative ethics is concerned with what is right, good, and obligatory. The third kind of ethical inquiry is analytical, critical metaethics. It deals with the meaning of ethical terms, such as "good" or "right". It inquires if and how one can justify ethical judgments. It wants to know what is the nature of morality, and what is the meaning of freedom and responsibility.[12]

William Lillie in his *Introduction to Ethics* divided ethics into six disciplines: (1) descriptive or positive science of morals, describing what different people or societies consider to be moral behavior; (2) normative science of ethics, which is concerned with valid moral standards; (3) moral philosophy, which examines the validity of ethical standards by determining their place in the universe; (4) casuistry, which applies ethics to concrete cases; (5) moralizing or practical ethics with the aim of improving conduct; and (6) the art of good life.[13]

This six-part division of ethics is applicable to Jewish ethics. There is an entire genre of Jewish literature on (5), practical ethics. Many of these writings have proven to be very popular among the people and have gone through many editions and translations.[14] They received additional significance with the birth of the Musar movement initiated by Rabbi Israel Lipkin of Salant (1810–1883) and his followers, who encouraged the thorough reading and rereading of them.

Illustrative of the fourth category, casuistry, are the many concrete problems of an ethical nature that are brought to rabbis and other wise men for their opinions or halachic decisions concerning them. Some of these ethical problems are ordinary and some are quite complex, such as those dealing with bioethics or capital punishment.[15]

Ethics as a branch of philosophy, although dealing with human conduct and a practical matter, is concerned mainly with categories (2) and (3) cited by Dr. Lillie. He believed that "ethics is primarily a part of the quest for truth and the motive of studying it is the desire for knowledge."[16]

Harold Titus in *Ethics for Today* defined the subject as "the study of human conduct insofar as that conduct may be considered right or wrong."[17] He maintained that ethical systems and human conduct must be "appraised and criticized,"[18] and that ethics has to clarify why one act is better than another.[19] Professor Titus believed that ethics seeks out the most intelligent principles of behavior required for a most wholesome life, and searches to point out life's true values.[20]

Some of the philosophical problems that are the concern of ethics include: What is meant by basic ethical terms such as "good," "right," "ought," "justice," etc.? What is the highest good (*summum bonum*)? Are there any all-inclusive, general principles that can offer guidance for proper ethical living? How can one determine what is ethical? What is the relationship between ends and means and between deeds and motives? How are ethics and religion or ethics and law related to each other?

PRINCIPLES OF JEWISH ETHICS

A major aspiration of philosophical ethics is to discover a general principle that could serve as an overall guide for ethical conduct. Two such helpful principles enunciated by philosophers include the categorical imperative of Immanuel Kant and the utilitarian principle of the greatest good for the greatest number.

There are several statements with philosophical implications in rabbinic literature that can provide us with sweeping guidelines for proper moral behavior. The first is the maxim of Hillel (end of first century B.C.E. and beginning of first century C.E.), "What is hateful unto you, do not unto your neighbor,"[21] sometimes referred to as the negative golden rule. Two related comprehensive formulas are found in the *Sifra*[22] on the Biblical verse "Love your fellow as yourself."[23] Rabbi Akiva (second century C.E.) called the verse a comprehensive rule in the Torah ("*klal gadol baTorah*"). Ben Azzai, a contemporary of Rabbi Akiva, believed that a more comprehensive dictum is found in the verse "This is the record of Adam's line—When God created man, He made him in the likeness of God."[24]

Dr. Max Kadushin (1895–1980) asserted that "Rabbinic literature does not contain all-inclusive, general ethical principles, nor was there any attempt to formulate such principles."[25] He did aver that Rabbi Akiva's statement stresses the value concept of love and Ben Azzai's the value concept of man.[26] Without attempting to argue for or against Dr. Kadushin's views, it could still be affirmed with at least some justification that philosophical lessons can be derived from rabbinic teaching because rabbinic texts, particularly agadic ones similar to biblical texts, are multidimensional and exude interpretations and meanings that illuminate our understanding on many different levels, including the philosophical.

Ben Azzai's accentuating the concept of man and his creation in the divine image is another indication that Jewish ethics is not parochial, but relates to all mankind. According to Ben Azzai, it would seem that since all men have descended from Adam and have a likeness to God, it is our duty and obligation to treat each and every person with respect and dignity and as an end in himself or herself. This position has a strong Kantian flavor.

Rabbi Akiva undoubtedly also had a very high regard for mankind. However, he also looked to the heart in our relations with other people. He would esteem all people as having divine qualities and worthy of our obligation to treat them as ends in themselves, but he was not satisfied with mere intellectual ethics emanating from duty alone. Instead, he presented a sympathetic ethic that emanates from love.

An example: Moshe is in need of a favor, and asks his friend Joe for help. Joe really does not want to be bothered. Maybe he is occupied with other interests? Nevertheless, his conscience tells him that he is obligated or has a duty to come to Moshe's aid, even though he really does not have his heart in the matter. When Moshe realizes that Joe considers the help offered as merely an obligation and a great sacrifice, he would rather forego the favor. He would prefer assistance that comes more from love than from obligation. In this instance, precedence is given to an ethic of "Love your fellow man" over an ethic based on "This is the record of Adam's line."

Another example: Marcia asks her friend Rachel for a favor. She is happy to come to Marcia's aid. Rachel loves Marcia, and besides she has nothing of great importance on the agenda at the moment. Rachel runs eagerly to help. Is Rachel's eagerness to come to the rescue so noble if it requires no sacrifice on her part, no feeling of obligation, if the act on her part originates from the heart and not from the mind? In this instance, a higher premium might be placed on Ben Azzai's principle over Rabbi Akiva's. Apparently there is room for both maxims and both can serve as general, comprehensive guidelines toward proper ethical understanding and conduct.[27]

MOTIVES AND DEEDS IN JEWISH ETHICS

These remarks about motives lead to an exploration of the relationship between motives and deeds, and whether one has priority over the other in Jewish philosophy. It is inaccurate to refer to Judaism as a religion of deed and not of creed. However, there is no question that deeds occupy a central position within the Jewish religion, as the concept of *mitzvah* clearly indicates. Performing *mitzvot*, though, should not be confused with "religious behaviorism" or "pan-halachic theology," using Professor Abraham Joshua Heschel's felicitous phraseology.[28] The Talmud raises the question whether deeds are performed adequately if proper intention is lacking?[29] Is the deed sufficient without the thought behind the deed? Rabbi Bachya Ibn Pakuda's *The Duties of the Heart* (late eleventh century) accentuates the significance of religious inwardness and its role in the performance of *mitzvot*.

In his theory of ethics, Kant maintained that the quintessential ingredient of an ethical act is the motive behind it. It is essential that an ethical act be performed out of a sense of duty or as a principle of the will that conforms to reason.[30] On the surface, it appears that this is also the Jewish view, considering the important role ascribed to *mitzvot*. Indeed, the rabbis tell us that "he who is commanded and fulfills [the command] is greater than he who fulfills it though not commanded."[31] Thus, both Jewish teaching and Kant stress obligation. There is nevertheless a crucial difference between them. Whereas a Kantian is duty bound to the "moral law within," Judaism obligates its adherents to the Divine law above.

Does this mean that Judaism rejects an independent ethic, one divorced from religion? Not at all! First, there is no rejection of the person who acts morally or properly without being commanded. The only claim being made is that he or she is not as great as one who acts because God commanded it. Second, we find incidents in the Bible where man is held responsible for his moral acts even without the Divine command. The most obvious example is the punishment of Cain for having killed his brother Abel, even though the prohibition against murder had not yet been promulgated.[32] A third indication of the autonomy of ethics is the observation of Rabbi Yochanan (ca.180–ca.279), "If the Torah had not been given we could have learned modesty from the cat, honesty from the ant, chastity from the dove, and good manners from the cock."[33]

ETHICS AND RELIGION

If ethics is an independent activity with its own valid standards, where and why does religion fit in? Bearing on this, it is often inquired whether something is good because God wills it, or God wills it because it is good? Is it possible for God to will something that is evil? Medieval philosophers questioned whether God is able to do that which is impossible, and if not, whether this limits His omnipotence? Rabbi Saadia Gaon (882–942) opposed those who require that an omnipotent God be able to do the logically impossible like bring back yesterday in its original condition or cause the number five to be more than ten without adding to the former. He maintained that making such requirements of God is tantamount to ascribing absurdity to God.[34] In Jewish thinking, it is also absurd to believe that God wills that which is evil. God and evil are antitheses. Where there is one you do not have the other.

Nonetheless, it is true that Judaism recognizes the existence of evil and that some of it is created by God. It is written in Isaiah,

> I form the light, and create darkness;
> I make peace, and create evil;
> I am the Lord, that doeth all these things.[35]

The fact that evil has been brought into existence by God serves as an indication that it is not absolute, does not exist by itself and of necessity, and consequently can ultimately be vanquished, even if we do not understand exactly and precisely how.

The book of Job offers some insight into this antinomy of the existence of God Who is divorced from evil and Who is also the creator of evil. The book was not included in the Bible to enunciate ethical skepticism or to assert that God does not treat Job or mankind fairly. It does purport to teach us that since God exists, evil cannot triumph. In the book, Job takes the offensive in tackling the difficult problem of theodicy. He challenges God about why he suffers torment although he is righteous. When God finally replies to Job out of the tempest, He does not really offer a justification for Job's suffering, yet Job is satisfied, and he says,

> I have heard You with my ears,
> But now I see You with my eyes;
> Therefore, I recant and relent,
> Being but dust and ashes.[36]

Why was Job satisfied after he witnessed God's presence even though he received no justification from Him for his original complaint? The answer is that God's presence alone is sufficient, for if God is there then evil is not—even if we do not and cannot understand. Job's recanting and relenting when he receives the theophany, even without a Divine explanation, are a clear indication that God and evil are mutually exclusive. God, by His mere presence, may be perceived as a "Guarantor" of ethics, to use the terminology of Hermann Cohen (1842–1918).[37]

So far we still have not expounded the role of religion in ethics or answered whether it is needed, especially if ethics is considered an independent inquiry. It is generally accepted that there are three noble goals to be pursued in human life: the beautiful, the true, and the good. The first is acquired largely through the arts, the second via the sciences and philosophy, and the third by ethical conduct, which includes good deeds performed with the highest motives and intentions. Judaism teaches that there is a fourth goal, one that is higher than the other three and also subsumes them. This fourth goal is holiness, as pronounced by the Biblical verse, "You shall be holy, for I, the Lord your God, am holy."[38] Holiness here implies *imitatio Dei*, and imitating God entails proper ethical conduct. This is illustrated by Abba Shaul's (mid-second century) interpretation of the verse "This is my God and I will glorify Him."[39] The verse, according to him, means, "Be like Him. Just as He is gracious and merciful, so be thou also gracious and merciful." [40] Rabbi Chama bar Chanina (third century) gave us another example of *imitatio Dei*, entailing ethical behavior: "After the Lord your God, ye shall walk." [41] "How can man walk after God? Is He not a consuming fire? What is meant is that man ought to imitate the attributes of God. Just as the Lord clothes the naked, so you shall clothe the naked. Just as He visits the sick, so you shall visit the sick, etc." [42]

Jewish ethics involves imitating the ways of the Holy God. It is ethics of holiness, which includes and encompasses goodness. This is why Jewish sources rarely place a line of demarcation between the commandments pertinent to ethics and those relating to ceremonies. Both are meant to guide the observer toward a life of holiness and emanate from the same source. Philosophical ethics aims for the good, while Jewish ethics, insofar as it is religious, aims for the holy.

ETHICS AND HALACHA

The Jewish moral law has traditionally found its expression within the Halacha, or the Jewish legal system, which, of course, contains many other laws besides ethical ones. The relationship of ethics and law is an intricate one. Supreme Court Justice Oliver Wendell Holmes distinguished between a court of law and one of ethics. He fought against any confusion of law and morals. He believed if any member of the court began talking about justice, he was shirking his duty to think in legal terms. [43] This attitude of Justice Holmes is contrary to the spirit of Jewish law, which has its own legal methodology. Divorcing ethics from a God-given law is a contradiction in terms, and is totally alien from Jewish thinking. While the Halacha deals with *nonethical* subject matter, it unequivocally rejects anything *unethical*.

Despite this, it was recognized that it is possible to obey the Halacha according to the letter, and still remain a "scoundrel within the law." [44] Also, it was recognized that the law is not inclusive of all of life's conditions and minutiae. [45]

In order to provide correctives for these situations, several provisions have been introduced in an attempt to keep life situations and the ethical within the purview of the law. These provisions include the principle of equity, *Lifnim MiShurat HaDin*[46] (beyond the limit of the law), and the teachings "And thou shalt do that which is right and good,"[47] and "Her ways are ways of pleasantness."[48] Rabbi Aharon Lichtenstein claimed that these stipulations were introduced by the Halacha itself to fill in any lacunae that might exist in the law. These moral principles, though not an integral part of the body of the Halacha, were nonetheless created by it. Thus, the Halacha is complete, all-inclusive, and provides for a complete morality within the law.[49]

Before proceeding further, it is essential to note that many philosophers of the twentieth century have abandoned traditional ethical thought. Perhaps the most extreme of them is A. J. Ayer, who wrote, "As ethical judgments are mere expressions of feelings, there can be no way of determining the validity of any ethical systems, and, indeed no sense in asking whether any such system is true."[50] Charles L. Stevenson believed that ethics and judgments of value are expressions of attitudes that the holder evokes, or wishes to evoke, in others. Stevenson noted that attitudes are based on beliefs, and thus they can be reasoned about.[51]

This type of ethical thinking, even in its less extreme versions, detracts from philosophy's role of teaching general moral truths and offering practical guidance for human deportment and undoubtedly influences and is reflected by the ebb of morality prevalent in society as a whole. This situation alone makes it incumbent upon Jewish ethics to fill the vacuum left by philosophy.

Even if traditional ethics were intact, an ethics that is based upon religion has an essential task to perform. Ultimately, it must answer why should people not be selfish? Even if definite standards of proper behavior are accepted, what would prevent some people from cheating? What would deter a Nietzschean "ubermensch" from going "beyond good and evil?"[52] It is true that there are so-called pious individuals whose ethical conduct does not receive very high grades. However, Jewish teachings and the system of Halacha do provide motivation for moral living by presupposing the existence of God, who calls for ethical living and is its "Guarantor." The fear of Heaven can and undoubtedly does provide powerful stimuli for proper ethical behavior and is a deterrent against acting immorally.

THE ETHICAL PERSON

Our discussion has concentrated on the ethical deed or act. Now we shall focus on its performer, the ethical person. The distinction between them is not just a difference of subject and object. It is known that a scoundrel can sometimes do something magnanimous, and an ethical individual something less than laudatory. Good intentions sometimes lead to evil results, as indicated by the oft-quoted saying, "The road to Hell is paved with the best intentions." It also happens, perhaps frequently, that people not notable for their honesty and integrity are philanthropists or civic leaders accomplishing much good for others. There is not always a perfect correlation between the ethical person and the ethical act.

We already presented some criteria and rules for discerning ethical behavior. Now our objective is to discover the qualities required of an ethical person, and how to develop and nurture them. Some thinkers maintain that this is the primary concern and goal of ethics. Plato and Aristotle seem to view morality this way, as they wrote more of virtues and the virtuous than of what is right and obligatory.[53]

When dealing with desirable moral traits, philosophy does not try to provide us with a list of all the virtues that may come to mind. Rather, it presents us with cardinal virtues—that is, virtues that cannot be derived from others and from which the others are derived.[54] Plato thought that there are four cardinal virtues: wisdom, courage, temperance, and justice.[55] The enumeration of virtues, whether cardinal or more detailed, not only gives us a useful description of the ethical personality, but also serves as a helpful pedagogical instrument for providing ethical training to children, students, and interested adults.

The famous *braita*[56] of Rabbi Pinchas ben Yair lists primary virtues that are esteemed within Judaism. The listing of virtues found in this

Braita, also called the "Saint's Progress," [57] formed the structure of Rabbi Moses Chaim Luzzatto's (1707–1746) popular ethical treatise, *Mesillat Yesharim*. The *Braita* reads as follows: "Rabbi Pinchas ben Yair says: Torah [study or knowledge of Torah] brings to precision, precision brings to alacrity, alacrity brings to cleanliness, cleanliness brings to abstention, abstention brings to purity, purity brings to saintliness [*chassidut*], saintliness brings to humility, humility brings to fear of sin, fear of sin brings to holiness, holiness brings to the [possession of] the holy spirit, the holy spirit brings to eternal life [resurrection of the dead], and saintliness is greater than any of these." [58]

The anonymous popular ethical work, *Orchot Tzadikim* (The Ways of the Righteous), also known as *Sefer HaMidot* (Book of Ethics or Virtues), has as its purpose to improve the qualities of the soul and to inculcate the fear of God. The author believed that the acquisition of good qualities or virtues is not sufficient to lead a person to proper conduct unless he also possesses the fear of Heaven. The latter "is the bond that joins the virtues into one harmonious whole, and is like the thread that holds together a string of pearls. The moment you loosen the thread, the pearls scatter, and likewise if you are lax in the matter of the fear of God, the virtues will become ineffective. And when man possesses virtues, he is likely to observe the Torah and its precepts." [59] Twenty-five chapters of the *Orchot Tzadikim* are devoted to various virtues and vices, and offer the reader practical advice concerning them.

The Musar movement, founded in the nineteenth century by Rabbi Israel Salanter, set as its goal to train individuals to become ethical people of the highest caliber, which entails the cultivation of the various virtues. It was recognized by the Musarniks that acquiring virtues differs from acquiring scientific knowledge. The latter is an intellectual pursuit, whereas the former, as was already recognized by Aristotle, is also a matter of instilling good habits in the area of morality. [60] Becoming an ethical person, as required by the Musar movement, demands long, continuous study with a great deal of critical self-examination. Pietistic literature like Rabbi Bachya Ibn Pakuda's *Duties of the Heart* and the *Mesillat Yesharim* were studied over and over, with each word articulated carefully, loudly, and with much enthusiasm, so that the ethical teachings should penetrate the heart and soul. Frequently students kept diaries recording their activities and suggestions on how to improve upon them. They were also guided and influenced by special teachers (*mashgichim*) affiliated with Musar *klausen* and *yeshivot* who taught and lectured on appropriate ethical subject matter. The virtues regarded highly by Musar include: peacefulness, patience, orderliness, diligence, modesty, righteousness, frugality, alacrity, silence, self-control, and truth.[61]

Aristotle and later Maimonides expounded a theory of virtue based upon adopting the mean, or the position in between two opposite types of behavior, both of which are undesirable. Virtuous activity is moderation between over indulgence and over suppression of any act. Aristotle provided a long list of moral triads of virtuous means and wrong extremes. For example, courage is the proper mean between wrongful cowardice and rashness. Liberty is the proper mean between stinginess and prodigality.[62] Maimonides in his *Mishneh Torah*[63] cited an exception to this principle of the mean, and asserted that when it comes to pride and humility, one must avoid the middle way and always be very humble, as Moses our teacher was not only humble, but *very* humble;[64] and as our sages commanded, "Be very, very lowly of spirit."[65] In this context it should be mentioned that Rabbi Solomon Ibn Gabirol (ca.1020–ca.1057) and Rabbi Bachya Ibn Pakuda regarded humility as the highest quality of the soul, the highest virtue.[66]

Rabbi Joseph B. Soloveitchik (1903–1993) in a lecture declared that living according to the so-called golden mean does not entail a static concept, that one must always act the same way regardless of any circumstances. There are times when it is proper to depart from the middle path and, if the situation warrants, to adopt an extreme position. However, one must be in control and know when to utilize the extremes, and to limit such usage only to those occasions when the mean is an inappropriate response.[67]

It is a task of philosophy to generalize by reducing particulars to their least common denominator. Much of our discussion has centered around the ethical deed and the ethical person, on justice, equity, and virtue, with humility being the highest virtue according to some think-ers. The exalted, often-quoted teaching of the prophet Micah is perhaps a summary statement of our theme:

> He has told you, O man, what is good,
> And what the Lord requires of you,
> Only to do justice
> And to love kindness,
> And to walk modestly with your God.[68]

ETHICS AND TORAH

A topic sometimes dealt with by ethicists is the relationship of ethics and knowledge. Socrates taught that virtue *is* knowledge, for if a person knows what is good for him, he will refrain from harming himself and conse-quently will adhere to the moral life.[69] Spinoza (1632–1677) is another philosopher who taught ethical rationalism. The good life, according to him, consists of knowing, living according to, and loving God—Who for Spinoza, a pantheist, is identified with nature and its laws.

It is true that there is a rational tendency and a need for knowledge within Jewish ethics. Jewish ethics requires living according to the moral precepts contained in the Torah and in rabbinic literature and requires that one be aware of these sources. Although Judaism has an intellectual side to its ethical thought, it also has an affective, sympathetic compo-nent. Judaism recognizes that man does not live by reason alone. This is most clearly illustrated by the notion of the *Yetzer HaRa*, or evil im-pulse, which provides reason and the good impulse with a formidable opponent in the battle for control of the psyche. In other words, there are a number of factors that influence and sometimes govern human behavior, and reason is only one of them.

The rabbis offer some recommendations for a person to gain control over the evil impulse. They include study of Torah, prayer, and as a last resort, reflection upon the day of death.[70] "The Holy One, blessed be He, said to Israel: My children, I have created the evil impulse, and

I have created the Torah as an antidote to it; if you occupy yourselves with Torah, you will not be delivered into its power."[71] "If this despicable thing [the evil impulse] meets you, drag it along to the house of study."[72] Even though the study of Torah is a prophylactic and a remedy against the triumph of the evil instinct, the battle is not that simple because the evil *yetzer* attacks scholars most of all, as an old man related to Abaye (278–338): "He who is greater than his neighbor, his *yetzer* is also greater."[73]

One might speculate what it is about Torah study that acts as an antidote or remedy against the evil urge? Is it simply a substitute activity, a distraction of the mind, an act of sublimation by way of the highest level of intellectual activity? Or is the study of Torah a supreme religious activity, an occupation immersed in holiness, that enables it to act as a counterforce, a powerful weapon in the combat against temptation?

MEANS AND ENDS

A subject discussed in ethical literature is the interaction between means and ends, whether and when one justifies the other. Niccolo Machiavelli's *The Prince* is the classic statement of the position that the end justifies the means. His book is a political guide for the success of a ruler, who is permitted to use immoral tactics skillfully to his or her advantage. It should be noted that although Machiavelli allowed immoral means for a ruler to gain an end, he thought that moral corruption in a people does not make for good government.[74]

The other side of the question can also be debated: whether the means can justify the end? For example, a person might be preoccupied with worthwhile community service, but thereby neglects the needs of his or her own household. An individual might be studying Torah almost constantly, but on account of it may be slack in his or her responsibilities toward others and to the community at large. Here we wonder whether lofty means always justify the ends that they produce?

The American Pragmatist John Dewey, in his treatment of this issue, connected means and ends. He asserted that ends cannot be accepted in isolation without a consideration of the means. Means and ends are never independent of each other.[75]

The rabbis deal with this issue when they inform us that a stolen *lulav* is invalid. They present us with the principle of *Mitzvah Habaa BeAveira*, a commandment made possible through a transgression is unacceptable.[76] Dr. Joseph Schechter wrote "One cannot fulfill a commandment with a stolen object. He who recites a blessing on this reviles God, for how could he utter, 'Who has sanctified us with His commandments' while the stolen object is in his hand."[77]

VALUE OF HUMAN LIFE

An interesting ethical question that took on awesome dimensions in the dark 1940s has to do with the value of one person's life vis-a-vis another person's life or in connection with the lives of many people or an entire community. There is a well-known Talmudic discussion centering around the Biblical words "That your brother may live with you."[78] The *Gemara* states, "If two are traveling on a journey [far from civilization], and one has a pitcher of water, if both drink, they will [both] die, if only one drinks, he can reach civilization. The Son of Petura taught: It is better that both should drink and die, rather than that one should behold his companion's death. Until Rabbi Akiva came and taught: 'that your brother may live with you.' thy life takes precedence over his life."[79]

This difference of opinion between Rabbi Akiva and Ben Petura takes on an unexpected twist when we recall that Rabbi Akiva is the one who taught that "Love your fellow as yourself" is a comprehensive rule of the Torah. Perhaps we would have expected him to advocate sharing the water with his fellow? However, it was Ben Petura who took the seemingly equalitarian position. And what is more, according to the *Ritva*, he seemingly does so on the basis of that very same verse of "Love your fellow as yourself."[80] However, we need not view Rabbi Akiva as wavering in his position of the centrality of "Love your fellow as yourself." It simply means that he predicates one's own existence as a prerequisite for loving one's neighbor, or for having the capability of loving him or her. He might say, "I am, therefore I love."

That Judaism places a high premium on the worth of an individual is evident from the fact that it is forbidden to sacrifice one single Jew in order to save an entire group. In the words of Maimonides, "If idolaters said to men: 'Give us one of you to be killed or we will kill all,' all must be killed rather than surrender an Israelite soul."[81]

This choice of sacrificing one life or several lives in order to save many more was no mere theoretical discussion in the European ghettos during World War II. Members of the Judenrat, the ghetto governments run by Jews but established by the Nazis to carry out their infamous policies, had to decide this and similar life and death predicaments. Frequently, the members of the Jundenrat consulted the rabbis who resided in the various ghettos concerning these harrowing ethical and religious situations, and the above-quoted passage from Maimonides' work served as a focal point of the considerations and deliberations, the agreement and dissent.

When Jacob Gens surrendered part of the Vilna community to the Nazis, hoping thereby to rescue the remainder of Jews, the rabbis of Vilna sent a delegation to inform him that he was violating Jewish law, and in support of their position they cited Maimonides' view. Rabbi Abraham Duber Shapiro of Kovna fainted when he was asked whether the Judenrat should comply with the Nazi request to hand over Jews who were unsuitable for hard labor. After he was convinced that resistance would be futile and might result in the death of all, he replied, "If a Jewish community (may God help it) has been condemned to physical destruction, and there are means of rescuing part of it, the leader of the community should have courage and assume the responsibility to act and rescue what is possible." Similarly, Rabbi Yitzchak Groysman spoke on behalf of his fellow rabbis in Bedzin in support of Moshe Merin's position that Jews should be delivered to the Nazis for transportation by force in the hope that many more would be saved. Rabbi Groysman affirmed that Merin's suggestion opposed Jewish ethics and religion. However, since each Jewish household faced a great calamity, there was no other way but to choose the lesser evil.[82]

Another mind-boggling ethical dilemma of those horrible days concerns the Judenrat in general. Which is preferable: to accept Judenrat membership entailing collaboration with the Nazis, but with the hope of somewhat ameliorating the dreadful position of the ghetto Jews; or to avoid the profane alliance with the devil and let the Nazis do their own dirty work, even if it meant more suffering for the ghetto residents?

Ethics is an inquiry that is concerned with personal improvement and how one is to act properly toward one's fellow man. During the Holocaust period, Jewish ethics dealt with the conundrum of how to be a *mensch* while living with beasts and how to be worthy of heaven while incarcerated in hell.

ENDNOTES

1. W. D. Ross, *Aristotle* (New York: Meridian Books, 1959), p. 183.

2. Leo Rosten, *Treasury of Jewish Quotations* (New York: Bantam Books, 1977) p. 451.

3. Gen. 18:23–25. Although the situations varied, Abraham and Job preceded Rabbi Levi Yitzchak of Berditchev (ca.1740–1810) in directly pleading to and outright challenging God concerning matters of ethics. Rabbi Levi Yitzchak is known as the great defender of the Jewish people before God.

4. Deut. 16:20.

5. Lev. 19:18; Sifra, Kedoshim on this verse.

6. See I Sam. 15:22 and Amos 5:21–24.

7. Is. 1:26–27.

8. Hos. 2:21–22.

9. For rabbinic views of ethics, see such works as A. Cohen, *Everyman's Talmud* (New York: E. P. Dutton, 1949); Max Kadushin, *Worship and Ethics* (New York: Bloch, 1963); C. G. Montefiore, and H. Loewe, *A Rabbinic Anthology* (Cleveland, and New York: Meridian and Philadelphia: Jewish Publication Society, 1963); George Foot Moore, *Judaism*, vol. II, (Cambridge: Harvard University Press, 1927); Solomon Schechter, *Aspects of Rabbinic Theology* (New York: Macmillan, 1909; New York: Schocken, 1961); and Ephraim E. Urbach, *Chazal* (Jerusalem: Magnes Press, 1971 [In Hebrew; English translation by Israel Abrahams is available]).

10. Nathan Rotenstreich, *Jewish Philosophy in Modern Times* (New York: Holt, Rinehart and Winston, 1968), p. 6.

11. From remarks made by Rabbi Reuvain Feinstein shortly after the passing of his father, Rabbi Moshe Feinstein.

12. William Frankena, *Ethics* (Englewood Cliffs, NJ: Prentice-Hall, 1963), p. 4.

13. William Lillie, *An Introduction to Ethics* (London and New York: University Paperbacks, 1961), p. 14.

14. Titles of three such works on Jewish practical ethics are: *Chovot HaLevavot*, by Rabbi Bachya Ibn Pakuda; *Shaarei Teshuva*, by Rabbi Jonah Gerondi; and *Mesillat Yesharim*, by Rabbi Moshe Chaim Luzzatto.

15. Three volumes concerned with such topics are: (1) Fred Rosner and J. David Bleich, eds., *Jewish Bioethics*, (New York: Sanhedrin Press, 1979); (2) Fred Rosner, *Modern Medicine and Jewish Ethics* (Hoboken, NJ: Ktav and Yeshiva University, 1986); (3) Basil F. Herring, *Jewish Ethics and Halakhah For Our Time* (Hoboken, NJ: Ktav and Yeshiva University, 1984).

16. Lillie, op. cit., p. 18.

17. Harold H. Titus, *Ethics For Today* (Boston: American Book Co., 1936), p. 5.

18. Ibid., p. 6.

19. Ibid., p. 5.

20. Ibid., pp. 6–7.

21. Shab. 31a.

22. Sifra, Kedoshim to Lev. 19:18.

23. Lev. 19:18.

24. Gen. 5:1.

25. Kadushin, op. cit., p. 31.

26. Ibid., p. 34.

27. Ibid., pp. .31–37; 242–243, notes 60–66.

28. Abraham Heschel, ch. 29 of *Between God and Man*, ed. Fritz A. Rothschild (New York: Free Press, 1959).

29. Ber. 13a; Pes. 114b; R. H. 28b.

30. Titus, op. cit., p. 46.

31. Kid. 31a; B. K. 38a; B. K. 87a.

32. See Yitzchak Heinemann, *Taamei HaMitzvot BiSafrut Yisrael*, vol. I (Jerusalem: HaMador HaDati LeInyenei HaNoar ViHeChalutz shel HaHistadrut HaTzionit, 1954), p. 14.

33. Eruvin, 100b.

34. Saadia Gaon, *The Book of Beliefs and Opinions* (New Haven: Yale University Press, 1948), pp. 25, 134.

35. Is. 45:7.

36. Job 42:5–6.

37. Eva Jospe, "Introduction," in Eva Jospe, Translator and Editor, *Reason and Hope: Selections From the Writings of Hermann Cohen,* (New York: Norton, 1971), p. 21. For an excellent thought-provoking anthology of various interpretations of the Book of Job, see Nahum N. Glatzer, ed., *The Dimensions of Job* (New York: Schocken, 1969).

38. Lev. 19:2.

39. Ex. 15:2.

40. Mechilta, Shira, 3.

41. Deut. 13:5.

42. Sota 14a. For expositions of *imitatio Dei* and of holiness and ethics, see Solomon Schechter, *Aspects of Rabbinic Theology* (New York: Schocken, 1961), ch. XIII. See also Seymour Siegel, "Imitation of God," in *Encyclopedia Judaica,* vol. 8, pp. 1292–1293. Rabbi Joseph B. Soloveitchik, in his discussion of *imitatio Dei,* distinguished between possessing certain divine attributes with an *adjective* connotation and acting according to them in a *verbal* sense. In the Sifrei, Eikev, walking in God's ways entails actually being merciful and gracious (*chanun virachum,* which are adjectives). In Sota 14a, the Talmud teaches us that to walk in God's ways, one should clothe the naked, visit the sick, etc. Whereas the talmudic passage instructs us to *act* Godly, the Sifrei wants us to *be* Godly; the former points to the activity, while the latter teaches inwardness. Rabbi Soloveitchik, in the same lecture, inquired what is the purpose of the prophetic writings? They do not enunciate new laws not already found in the Torah. Besides their function of admonishing, the prophets teach the ways of God and our obligation to pursue them. "Prophecy comes to instruct man how to participate in the qualities of God and to be worthy of His attributes." See Rabbi Joseph B. Soloveitchik, "Belnyan Mechikat HaShem," in *Shiurim LiZeicher Abba Mari Zal* vol. 2, (Jerusalem 1985), pp. 170–173.

43. Harold J. Berman, "Philosophical Aspects of American Law," In *Talks on American Law,* ed. Harold J. Berman (New York: Vintage, 1961), pp. 229–230.

44. Nachmanides (1194–1270), commentary to Lev. 19:2.

45. Ibid., commentary to Deut. 6:18; see also Magid Mishna to Shecheinim 14:5 of Maimonides' *Mishneh Torah.*

46. B. M. 30b.

47. Deut. 6:18.

48. Prov. 3:17.

49. Aharon Lichtenstein, "Does Jewish Tradition Recognize an Ethic Independent of Halacha?" in *Modern Jewish Ethics*, ed. Marvin Fox (Columbus, OH: Ohio State Press, 1975), pp. 62–88. Reprinted in *Contemporary Jewish Ethics*, ed. Menachem Marc Kellner (New York: Sanhedrin Press, 1978), pp. 102–123. On the topic of morality and Jewish law, see Basil F. Herring, op. cit.; Saul Berman, "Law and Morality," in *Encyclopedia Judaica*, vol. 10, pp. 1479–1484; Boaz Cohen, "Law and Ethics in the Light of Jewish Tradition," in Boaz Cohen, *Jewish and Roman Law*, Vol. 1, (New York: Jewish Theological Seminary, 1966), pp. 65–121.

50. Alfred Jules Ayer, *Language, Truth, and Logic* (London: Gollancz, 1951), p. 112.

51. Frankena, op. cit., p. 89.

52. Emil G. Hirsch, "Ethics," in *The Jewish Encyclopedia*, vol. 5, (New York: Ktav Publishing Company), (No Publication Date) Reprint of *The Jewish Encyclopedia*, (New York: Funk & Wagnalls, 1901–1905), p. 257.

53. Frankena, op. cit., p. 49.

54. Ibid., p. 50.

55. Plato, *Republic*, book IV. Dr. Max Kadushin referred to idolatry, murder, and adultery as three cardinal sins so considered by Judaism. See his *Worship and Ethics*, op. cit., pp. 223, 228. Concerning these sins, one should rather suffer martyrdom than perform them (San. 74a).

56. A *braita* is a tannaitic teaching of the mishnaic period that was excluded from the text of the Mishna.

57. See note no. 8 on p. 106 of Soncino Talmud, A. Z. 20b.

58. A. Z. 20b. See also Sot. 9:15 with commentary in Art Scroll Mishna.

59. *Orchot Tzadikim*, introduction. For a description of the book, see Meyer Waxman, *A History of Jewish Literature*, vol II, (New York: Bloch, 1943), pp. 280–282.

60. Aristotle, *Nicomachean Ethics*, book II, ch. 1. Since morality is learned through habit, and one learns to be moral and immoral during childhood—in the process of growing up, before a person can reason or philosophize—what is the purpose of philosophical discourse in the realm of ethics? Why study ethics post facto? One is or can be ethical without philosophy. The situation is similar to language and grammar. What is the purpose of studying grammar if

we learn to speak, write, and use language before we know its rules and structure? Why study grammar post facto? The answer is that it is necessary to know grammar in order to know language. Grammar sets the standards for proper linguistic usage. Thus, one can correct poor language habits, enabling one to utilize the language medium correctly and more effectively. In a similar manner, philosophical ethics aids a person toward an understanding of proper moral behavior and provides criteria and guidelines for improving one's own ethical behavior and for teaching morality to children, who learn from adults.

61. Israel Zissel Rabinowitz, "Mussar Movement," in *Otzar Yisrael Encyclopedia* (New York: Hebrew Publishing Co., 1907–1913 Hebrew), vol. 6, pp. 126–127. The Musar student, with his strict ethical discipline, is somewhat reminiscent of the Stoic sage of old (Lihavdil).

62. Aristotle, op. cit., book II–IV, and Maimonides, *Shmona Prakim* (Introduction to Avot), Ch. 4.

63. Maimonides, *Mishneh Torah*, Hilchot Deiot, 2:3.

64. Num. 12:13.

65. Avot 4:4.

66. See article on "Ethics" in *The Jewish Encyclopedia*, vol. 5, p. 23.

67. I am indebted to my brother for having made Rabbi Soloveitchik's comment known to me.

68. Micah 6:8.

69. Henry Sidgwick, *Outlines of the History of Ethics* (Boston: Beacon Press, 1886; citation is from 1931 edition), pp. 24–25.

70. Ber. 5a.

71. Kid. 30b.

72. Ibid.

73. Suk. 52a. See also Montefiore and Loewe, op. cit., p. 302.

74. George H. Sabine, *A History of Political Theory* (New York: Holt, 1950) pp. 339–340.

75. John E. Smith, *The Spirit of American Philosophy* (New York: Galaxy Books, 1966), pp. 152–156.

76. Suk. 30a. See the commentary on Suk. 3:1 in the Art Scroll Mishna.

77. Joseph Schechter, *Otzar HaTalmud* (Tel Aviv: Dvir, 1984), p. 241.

78. Lev. 25:36.

79. B. M., 62a.

80. See note under "Iyunim" section in Adin Steinsaltz's edition of the Talmud, B. M., 62a.

81. Maimonides, *Mishneh Torah*, "Hilchot Yesodei HaTorah," 5:5.

82. Isaiah Trunk, *Judenrat* (New York: Scarborough Books, 1977), pp. 420–436. See also Daniel Landes, "Spiritual Responses in the Ghettos," in *Genocide*, ed. Alex Grobman and Daniel Landes (Los Angeles: Simon Wiesenthal Center, 1983) pp. 196–211; and Lucy S. Dawidowicz, *The War Against the Jews* (New York: Holt, Rinehart and Winston and Philadelphia: Jewish Publication Society, 1975), pp. 279–310.

FOUR

Jewish Law

The attitudes that people have toward law range from veneration all the way to disparagement. An example of the former is the remark that law "offers protection against tyranny on the one hand, and anarchy on the other; it is one of society's chief instruments for preserving both freedom and order."[1] Derision of the law is illustrated by the following ditty:

> The net of law is spread so wide,
> No sinner from its sweep may hide.
> Its meshes are so fine and strong,
> They take in every child of wrong.
> O wondrous web of mystery!
> Big fish alone escape from Thee?[2]

Whatever one's feelings regarding the law, almost everyone recognizes its necessity. Concerning this the Talmud states, "As fish die when they are out of water, so do people die without law and order."[3]

Law,[4] or Halacha, is an integral part of Judaism. It occupies a substantial portion of the Pentateuch and of both the Babylonian and Palestinian Talmuds. Actually, at least until recent times it is Jewish law that served as the cement that bound all Jews together throughout their long history and dispersion. In the words of Professor Zalman B. Rabinkoff (ca.1882–ca.1941), "It is lucky for Judaism that there are not two opinions in it as to decisive Halachic questions. Were it not for this unity regarding all the precepts governing our everyday conduct, Judaism would long ago have split into sects and groups. Thanks to such unity in matters of Halacha, the considerable differences in philosophical approach could have little effect upon us."[5]

Some of the problems that concern the philosophy of law include the following: What is meant by law? What is the origin of law and what are its purposes? How is law made and how is it interpreted? What are the sources of legal authority? How does ancient law fit in with modern society and its problems? What is meant by equity, and how do law and ethics relate to each other?[6] Jewish philosophy wants to know not only the purpose of Halacha in general, but also the significance of the various *mitzvot* or commandments. It also investigates the role of law in the general religious experience, and the relationship between the Halacha and Agada, the nonlegal teachings of rabbinic literature.

JOHN AUSTIN AND THE CONCEPT OF MITZVAH

What is meant by the word law? The English legal theorist John Austin defined law as a command. He wrote, "A law is a command which obligates a person or persons to a course of conduct."[7] The law proceeds from superiors and binds or obligates inferiors. The superiors have the might or power to affect others with evil or pain, thus forcing them through fear to conduct themselves according to the wishes of the superiors.[8] Accordingly, the command concept, with its corollaries of sanction, superiority, and obligation or duty, constitutes the key to Austin's view of jurisprudence.[9] At first appearance, it would seem that Austin's definition of law fits Jewish law like a glove. The focal point of Jewish law is the *mitzvah* which is a commandment from a superior, all-powerful God to an inferior people who have the duty and obligation to obey the Divine Lawgiver or face sanctions. Considering the notion of *mitzvah*, one would think that John Austin wrote perceptively about the nature of Jewish law.

MITZVAH AND HALACHA

Austin's definition and description of law, however illuminating, are not sufficient because a large part of the law has to do not so much with commands as with procedures, with rules, and with regulations.[10] This aspect of the law displays a great similarity to the concept of Halacha, the Hebrew word for the rabbinical legal system meaning "go," "walk," or "follow." Halacha provides the rules and regulations of the Jewish legal system and the proper way to follow them.

In actuality, Halacha is intricately related to the category of *mitzvah*. This is clearly illustrated by two works of Maimonides, the paramount Jewish philosopher and legal authority. He composed a work on the 613 biblical commandments, entitled *Sefer HaMitzvot*, and a compendium of the entire Halacha called *Mishneh Torah*. These two works are enmeshed one with the other. The former, besides enumerating the commandments, is a prolegomenon to the latter, insuring its comprehensiveness. According to Professor Isadore Twersky (1930–1997), Maimonides, in order to avoid any halachic omissions, "needed an exact and exhaustive list of commandments which provided the scaffolding for the *Mishneh Torah* and guarded against forgetfulness and omissions."[11]

The *Mishneh Torah*, the comprehensive code par excellence, was dependent upon and constructed around the *Sefer HaMitzvot*, the book of Divine Commandments. From this we can infer that the Halacha, with all its rules and regulations, emanates from the *mitzvot* or commandments of the sovereign God. Jewish law ultimately is a command from a sovereign Superior to inferiors who have the duty and obligation to live according to that law.

LEGAL REALISM AND JEWISH LAW

An entirely different view of the nature of law, one with a strong skeptical connotation, is presented by legal realism. The legal realists objected to the traditional view of law as a "complete and autonomous system of logically consistent principles, concepts, and rules."[12] They were preoccupied with the process of judicial decision, with how law is made. They maintained that legal decisions are not compelled and that choice is necessary at every step. They argued that judges are not socially neutral and that their private views influence their decision making. The realists believed that judges do not merely draw logical conclusions from a body of law but in fact make law, and they must know and say that they do. Legal realists generally endorsed Oliver Wendell Holmes's definition of law as "the prophesies of what the courts will do in fact,"[13] and were also influenced by Roscoe Pound's distinction between "law in books" and "law in action," which implied a close scrutiny of the actual operation of legal institutions.[14]

How do some of the views and insights of legal realism relate to Jewish law? Legal realism shifts the fulcrum of the law from its corpus to its interpretation. The law is what the courts say it is. It is not so much the constitution, codes, or judicial precedent as it is the decisions and rulings of the judges who are presently adjudicating or applying the law.

Several examples from Jewish law indicate how it also depends upon those who interpret it. First, there is the divergence of opinions within Jewish law. It is related, "When the disciples of Shammai and Hillel (first century C.E.) who had not served [their teachers] sufficiently multiplied, dissensions increased in Israel and the Torah became like two Torot."[15] Even if there were no differences in the law to begin with, dissension eventually did arise. The law is not static, but depends upon people.

Another example is the well-known incident concerning the "oven of Achnai," which Rabbi Eliezer declared clean and the Sages declared unclean. Even though a Heavenly Voice pronounced that the law is according to Rabbi Eliezer, Rabbi Joshua (both Rabbi Eliezer and Rabbi Joshua lived in the first and second century C.E. and were teachers of Rabbi Akiva) said, "It [the Torah] is not in heaven."[16] Rabbi Jeremiah interpreted that the Torah had already been given at Mount Sinai, and we pay no attention to a Heavenly Voice because it is written in the Torah, "After the majority must one incline."[17] It is reported that the Holy

One, Blessed Be He, laughed with joy concerning this matter and said, "My sons have defeated Me, My sons have defeated Me."[18] Here again we witness the importance of the human element in the making of law, even—mind you!—in Divine Law, and even after the announcement by the Divine Voice that the ruling of Rabbi Eliezer was the correct one.

Another indication of the importance of judge-made law in the Halacha is the statement "Yiftach in his generation is like Samuel in his genera-tion."[19] Even if the Yiftach-like judge is only a light weight legal scholar, he has the authority to render judgment as the presiding judge at a particular time. Obviously it is inconceivable that a highly qualified judge and a less competent one would reason in an identical manner and al-ways offer the same legal verdict. Yet the decision of both types of judges is acceptable and valid. This shows that a static, precise law gives way to the judge or interpreter who is currently occupying the bench.

Let us cite one more example of legal realism in action as it is appli-cable to Jewish law. Suppose a complicated litigation takes place between two parties or one asks a rabbi a complex question; is anyone really certain of the ruling in advance of its delivery? There is always an ele-ment of doubt and unpredictability in the judicial process even though the law theoretically provides for certainty, consistency, stability, and hence predictability.

According to legal realism, the judge is the leading figure in law. John Chipman Gray believed that since courts have the last word, "all law is judge-made law." He quoted Benjamin Hoadly, "Whoever hath an absolute authority to interpret any written or spoken laws, it is he who is truly the Law-giver to all intents and purposes, and not the person who first wrote or spoke them."[20]

It is of interest that within the Halacha, the judiciary occupies center stage. There is no provision for a legislature, no houses of parliament to initiate legislation in rabbinic law. God was the Legislator at Sinai. The rest is up to the judiciary to interpret and to the officers to enforce, as it is written, "Judges and officers shalt thou make thee in all thy gates."[21] It should also be noted that there is no talmudic provision for lawyers in the modern sense nor for a system of courts of appeal. There are, of course, distinctions between various types of courts, such as a three-judge court for civil law, a twenty-three-judge court for criminal law, and the great seventy-one-justice Sanhedrin in Jerusalem.[22]

Obviously, one cannot overemphasize the importance of the jurist or those rendering legal decisions in general jurisprudence and in Jewish law. However, in the American legal system the judiciary is counterbalanced by a legislative or lawmaking body. Within the Halacha, there is no lawmaking institution per se. Thus, Jewish courts or those who render halachic decisions are not "checked and balanced" by other branches of government, and seem to have more power or authority than the judiciaries of other legal systems.

On the other hand, since Jewish law is of Divine origin, halachic jurists undoubtedly feel a greater responsibility and need for fidelity to the Divine legislation and therefore might be strict constructionists in their legal interpretation and decision rendering. A judge might feel more at liberty to follow his or her own inclinations when interpreting human law than when interpreting law of Divine origin.

Since Halacha is Divine law, or at least law of Divine origin, those who interpret it and render decisions according to it have to be not only great legal scholars but also highly devout. The Jewish judge is himself part of the religious legal system, and he must embody it and reflect it, not merely know it. The guardian of the Halacha is part of the Halacha, and necessarily partakes of its sacredness.

Despite the central position of judges and courts in both general and Jewish law, it would be a mistake to interpret legal realism as nominalism, where the law exists merely in the minds of jurists or, in a Berkleyan sense, only when it is being interpreted. There is no question that there is law "out there," that law exists even if all judges take a vacation (and sometimes it seems that they do). Law exists even if there is no litigation on the court calender or if the judiciary is not currently pronouncing legal decisions. The insights of legal realism enable us to understand better the relationship of the law to those who interpret it and how the interpretations themselves become a part of the body of law. In this manner, the law and legal literature prosper and flourish.

The philosophy of law is divided into several legal theories and schools of thought. We already have touched upon analytical jurisprudence, represented by John Austin, and upon legal realism. Other theories of law include: (1) Divine law, (2) natural law, (3) historical jurisprudence, and (4) sociological jurisprudence. The first maintains that law comes from God; The second, that the primary source and sanctions of the law are reason and morality. The third explains law as a product of the historical development of a people's spirit and character. The fourth views law as a balancing of various interests, weighing the social consequences of alternative policies.[23]

Although the lines of demarcation are not rigidly drawn, it would be correct to assert that within contemporary Judaism, Orthodoxy stresses Divine law; the Conservative movement, which grew out of Zacharias Frankel's (1801–1875) Positive Historical School, puts the accent on historical jurisprudence; and Reform Judaism accentuates sociological jurisprudence. This is not to imply that each denomination rejects the other schools of jurisprudence in toto. For instance, Orthodoxy accepts the authority of custom (*minhag*) and shows a great reluctance to abandon customs. "Rabbi Tanchum ben Chanilai said: One should never break away from custom."[24] According to the *Shulchan Aruch*, "The custom of our fathers is equivalent to Torah."[25] The concept of custom forms an integral component in the thought of the historical school of jurisprudence. Its founder, Friedrick von Savigny, taught that law is formed by custom and popular faith, "by internal, silently operating powers, not by the arbitrary will of the lawgiver."[26] Orthodoxy also recognizes the validity of natural law, which would include the precepts of the Torah that are easily acceptable by reason, such as ethics and those laws that come under the category of *mishpatim*, or judgments. Lastly the Orthodox also accept the sociological theory of law Examples of such recognition include Hillel's introduction of the *prozbul*[27] to encourage pre-Shmita lending; the acceptance of the validity of the testimony of only one witness instead of the usual two in cases of *Aguna* (when a woman's husband is missing and not confirmed as either living or deceased); the *"Cherem* of Rabbeinu Gershom," prohibiting polygamy among Ashkenazic Jewry; and the various *gezeirot* and *takanot* introduced by Jewish legal authorities in a quasi-legislative fashion. The point is that although the three denominations utilize aspects of various schools of jurisprudence, each of the three does stress the views of a different school and can be characterized in its terms.

CLASSIFICATION OF JEWISH LAWS

Classification, or reduction of many topics into related smaller ones, is a useful tool for understanding, for orderliness of thought, and for intellectual clarity.[28] Many scholars have classified Jewish law into several divisions in an attempt at reducing multiplicity into several broad categories. Here are some ways that Jewish legal authorities and philosophers have classified the Jewish legal system: (1) positive and negative commandments; (2) laws regarding man's relations to God and toward one's fellow man; (3) ceremonial laws and civil laws; (4) biblical and rabbinic laws; (5) laws between God and man, between man and his household, and between man and the rest of mankind; (6) criminal and civil laws; (7) laws performed by hand, mouth, or heart; (8) duties of the heart and duties of the limbs; (9) individual or private precepts and communal ones; (10) those valid under all circumstances and those performed only in the Land of Israel or when the Temple existed; (11) laws applicable from birth to marriage and from marriage until death; (12) rational laws and revelational ones whose significance reason cannot determine.[29]

CODIFICATION OF JEWISH LAW

Needless to say, classification of the law is essential for its codification. The various Jewish codes have employed three different types of arrangements: (1) according to the order in which the various commandments appear in the Torah, as exemplified by the *Sefer Mitzvot Gadol* and the *Sefer HaChinuch*; (2) according to the order in which the laws appear in the Mishna, as in the code of Rabbi Issac Alfasi (Rif: 1013–1103); and (3) topical arrangement of the laws into various categories, such as Maimonides' *Mishneh Torah*, the *Tur*, and the *Shulchan Aruch*.

Jewish legal literature is generally divided into three major genres. The first is textual exegesis and novellae: In the process of interpreting rabbinic texts, whether on an elementary or a complex level, many legal problems and decisions emerge. The second genre is codes of Jewish law and the third is responsa, or answers to legal questions submitted to various halachic authorities for their opinions and decisions. There is also a much smaller legal literature dealing with methodology, history, dictionaries, and encyclopedias.[30]

Jewish law covers all areas of life: individual and societal, civil and criminal, ceremonial and religious. "Even more than any other legal system, Jewish law penetrated all nooks and corners of Jewish living."[31] The extensiveness of Jewish law is magnified when we take into account its long history from biblical times onward and the vast legal literature pertaining to it. With these considerations in mind, we can easily understand the desire—nay, the need—for the codification of Jewish law. It is generally the aim of codification to gather relevant legal material and present it in an orderly form making it more available to many people and providing precision, conciseness, and final legal authority. Theoretically, once a law code exists, legal decisions can be extrapolated from it through deductive reasoning.[32]

Because of the logical and precise nature of codification and the finality it instills into law, historical jurisprudence does not favor codifying law. It proposes a legal theory in which law grows organically with a people's or nation's development and is an expression of its *volksgeist.* Savigny delayed the movement toward codified legal systems. He opposed the adoption of a uniform German code and advocated the natural and unplanned growth of national law.[33]

Professor Boaz Cohen (1899–1968) believed that the purpose of the various legal codes was utilitarian and not authoritarian. He cited three such purposes: (1) the systemization of a huge body of rules in order to facilitate the finding of a law; (2) the determination of law stemming from conflicting opinions; and (3) the incorporation of new decisions and customs that accumulate during the course of time.[34]

Despite the usefulness of Professor Cohen's utilitarian approach, Jewish legal codes nevertheless do have an authoritative status. Many of their compilers intended them to be binding, and even more important, they were accepted as such by various Jewish communities. One who abides by the Halacha cannot just ignore the decisions of the *Mishneh Torah* or *Shulchan Aruch* on utilitarian grounds. The laws set down in these codes and in others cannot whimsically be abrogated or abandoned because they have a binding authority within the Halacha. Nonetheless, it is also true that there is a give-and-take between vital fluidity and codal finality. Professor Twersky wrote, "A code is a rational construction which captures and freezes as much as possible of a fluid, unpredictable, sometimes recalcitrant reality, but there is always a fluctuating residuum which must be confronted openly and freshly."[35] He asserted that "Total certitude, finality, unilateral formulation—this was a codificatory utopia never to be achieved."[36]

JEWISH RESPONSA

Another source of Jewish law is the responsa literature, the equivalent of precedent and case law. It is estimated that approximately three hundred thousand legal judgments and decisions are contained in rabbinic responsa, which are written answers by legal scholars to questions submitted to them.[37] Felix Frankfurter referred to judge-made law as retail law whereas legislatures make wholesale law. Obviously, judges occupy themselves with individual cases or single questions, and only as cases are referred to them. The responsa constitutes referential jurisprudence, not initiatory law, and deals with Halacha on a case-by-case basis. The legal opinions expressed in the responsa are not as authoritative as those in the major codes but they are highly influential, particularly regarding the applicability of Jewish law to new life situations such as recent developments in modern science and technology. Those rendering Halachic decisions are not necessarily bound by the reasoning and decisions of their predecessors or contemporaries—and frequently they do disagree with them—but "Judges are everywhere largely influenced by what has been done by themselves or their predecessors."[38]

Ethics and equity are also considered as sources of law.[39] The relationship between ethics and Halacha has been treated in the chapter on Jewish ethics. It should be mentioned here that a distinction is made between law and ethics in that law is concerned with overt acts and is external, whereas ethics deals with human character and is internal.[40] From a secular or human perspective, this distinction holds true. It is not feasible or even possible for a human court to adjudicate or administer punishment for a person's innermost thoughts or motives, but only for external behavior and overt violations of the law. But from a religious or theological point of view the inner/outer distinction becomes blurry. A religious Jew conceives of God as omniscient, and all of a person's acts, whether moral, legal, or ceremonial, as equally visible to God. This is the reason for the irony when a so-called pious person is lax in his ethical conduct, for according to the premises of his own religious outlook, his ethics are overt in the eyes of God as is the rest of his behavior.[41]

INWARDNESS AND HALACHA

As religious law, Halacha is concerned not only with deeds but also with inwardness.[42] An interesting question in this regard is the much-discussed nature of *kavana*, or intention, within Jewish law.[43] It is debated whether one has to have *kavana* in order to fulfill one's legal obligations when performing *mitzvot?* Some believe that the controversy concerning *kavana* applies only to those commandments requiring the performance of deeds or actions, and that *kavana* is certainly a requisite for those commandments stemming from thought or speech, such as prayer. In accord with the view that *mitzvot* do not require intention, some scholars, such as Rabbi Ezekiel Landau (1713–1793) and the Vilna Gaon (1720–1797), opposed reciting formulae such as "*Hinnini Muchan Umzuman,*" or "*LiShem Yichud*" (statements of intention) before performing commandments, as is the custom of hasidim and Kabbalists.[44] Despite the disagreement whether *mitzvot* performed without *kavana* possess legal validity, "All authorities agree that due *kavana* to perform such *mitzvot* is desirable."[45]

As a philosophical issue, it might be asked what is meant by *kavana?* Is it merely a legal term or does it have other ramifications? As a halachic term, *kavana* might be defined as "the intention of the person performing the action to do so with the explicit intention of fulfilling the religious injunction which commands the action."[46] Philosophically, or as a religious category, when we think of *kavana* we have in mind inwardness, how the person is affected in his or her innermost being. A different conception of *kavana* is found in Kabbalism. Kabbalists have taught that proper mystical intention has an effect not only upon the worshipper or religious adherent himself or herself, but also upon the outer earthly and heavenly universe at large. "Every mystical intention, or *kavana*, draws light to the corresponding supernal configurations and raises sparks from the broken vessels."[47]

As a central religious phenomenon, *kavana* undoubtedly has a dynamic overtone and is not a static concept. This is illustrated in two essays composed by Rabbi Joseph B. Soloveitchik. In his "Halachic Man" essay, Rabbi Soloveitchik cited an incident in which his father, Rabbi Moshe, turned to the Chabad Chassid who began to weep before he was to sound the *shofar* on Rosh HaShana and said to him, "Do you weep when you take the *lulav?* Why do you weep when you sound the *shofar?* Are not both commandments of God?"[48] Here apparently the Rav is extolling the rational cool of the halachic man as he performs the various commandments with calculated, cognitive intent. In another essay concerning repentance and *shofar*, Rabbi Soloveitchik presented an entirely different scenario. He described the terror and fear felt on Rosh HaShana indicated in the prayer "Uvchein Tein Pachdicha," "Put Your fear upon all whom You have made, Your dread upon all You have created." When a person hears the sounding of the *shofar*, he is like one struck by a storm, reacting instinctively, without indulging in any rationalizations. He feels alone in the tempest, terrified, and afraid of his Creator. This fear-arousing experience brought about by the sound of the *shofar* on Rosh HaShana is the experiential cause for prompting a person to repent.[49] Thus, we see two entirely different descriptions of the complex concept of *kavana*.

Even those who negate or minimize the need or requirement for *kavana* undoubtedly would deprecate the rote performance of *mitzvot*.[50] It is, nevertheless, a requirement to perform them even when one is disinclined to do so or does not have the proper intent or concentration at a given time. There is also the concept of studying or performing *mitzvot* "not for their own sake," which will eventually lead to action "for its own sake."[51] This idea is reminiscent of the James-Lange Theory in which bodily action precedes and causes mental affections and not the generally accepted converse. Examples of this theory cited by William James include that we are sorry because we cry and afraid because we tremble and not the other way around, as is the commonsense view.[52] In a similar manner, it happens frequently that the mere performance of *mitzvot* leads to proper *kavana* and intense religious experience. There are occasions when *kavana* precedes *mitzvah* performance and times when the doing of the *mitzvah* precedes and actually causes the desired *kavana*, and "Not for its own sake" leads to "For its own sake."

In a number of areas we have noticed dichotomies and contradictions coexisting legitimately. The concepts of the outward performance of deeds and the inner religious experience is one such example. In ethics, we inquire which has priority: the deed or the motive behind the deed? In education, we are concerned with teaching children and simultaneously teaching subject matter. It seems that there is constantly a dynamic force, an operating dialectic in life situations. Professor Heschel wrote about "a polarity which lies at the very heart of Judaism," citing as examples *kavana* and deed, regularity and spontaneity, uniformity and individuality, Halacha and Agada, love and fear, understanding and obedience, joy and discipline, the good drive and the evil drive, creed and faith, etc.

"Taken abstractly," he wrote, "all these terms seem to be mutually exclusive, yet in actual living they involve each other; the separation of the two is fatal to both."[53]

HALACHA AND AGADA

One of the polar concepts that merits our special attention is the relationship between Halacha and Agada, the legal and nonlegal aspects of rabbinic teaching. Professor Heschel affirmed that you cannot have one without the other.[54] It is erroneous to believe that the essence of Judaism consists exclusively of either Halacha or Agada. Their interrelationship is "the very heart of Judaism. Halacha without agada is dead, agada without halacha is wild."[55]

An important contribution concerning the nature of Agada and Halacha and their interface is found in the writings of Dr. Max Kadushin. He taught that the thought of the rabbis of the talmudic period was chiefly concerned with value concepts such as holiness, the kingdom of Heaven, charity, commandments, and prayer. These value concepts are not isolated in themselves but, rather, are organically related and interwoven with each other. He believed that all the value concepts emanate from and intertwine with four dominant concepts: *midat haDin* (judgment), *midat haRachamim* (mercy), Torah, and Israel. The Agada explicates these value concepts and extracts them through its *midrashic* interpretation of the Bible.[56] The Halacha is concerned with the same value concepts as the Agada, but its aim is to actualize and concretize them in one's daily life. Three illustrating examples are: (1) the laws of tithing for the poor, the community plate (*tamchuy*), and community chest (*kuppa*) are concretizations of the value concept of charity; (2) the public reading of the Torah during synagogue services is an acting out of the value concept of Torah study;[57] and (3) the recital of the benediction before eating bread is the halachic manifestation of the value concept of God's love for mankind and for the individual who recites the blessing.[58] According to Dr. Kadushin, Agada and Halacha are related, with the purpose of the law being to put the rabbinic worldview into common practice of the entire Jewish populace.

The purpose and goal of Jewish law has occupied thinkers past and present. Rabbi Joseph B. Soloveitchik, in his "Halakhic Man," distinguished between the Halachic man and *Homo religiosus.* Although Halachic man is also a *Homo religiosus,* they actually travel in opposite directions. The latter "starts out in this world and ends up in supernal realms; halakhic man starts out in supernal realms and ends up in this world. . . . Basically [*Homo religiosus*] is a romantic who chafes against concrete reality and tries to flee to distant worlds that will restore his spirits. . . . Halakhic man, however, takes up his position in this world and does not move from it. He wishes to purify this world, not to escape from it."[59] The Halacha endeavors to bring the Divine presence and holiness within the confines of space and time, in earthly existence. The goal of Halacha is to "bring down the higher realm to the lower world,"[60] to have heaven on earth. The Halacha is concerned with the empirical world, with problems of earthly life in all of its particulars, with such things as civil law, forbidden foods, marriage and divorce, *chametz* and *matzah,* etc. It is democratic in that it is directed to all of Israel and not only to the spiritual elite.[61]

There is an element of similarity between Rabbi Soloveitchik's concept of Halacha and what Dr. Max Kadushin called "normal mysticism," or the religious experience of the rabbis that was associated with ordinary daily living.[62] Normal mysticism is experience of God that requires no visions, locutions, or other sense phenomena. It is not restricted to particular individuals with special or unusual aptitudes or temperament, or with extraordinary psychological equipment.[63] Dr. Kadushin wrote, "The ordinary, familiar everyday things and occurrences . . . constitute occasions for the experience of God. Such things as one's daily sustenance, the very day itself, are felt as manifestations of God's lovingkindness, calling forth *berakot. Kedushah,* holiness, which is nothing else than the imitation of God, is concerned with daily conduct, with being generous and merciful, etc."[64] The features of normal mysticism make it possible for both the spiritual leader and the common man to have the same kind of experience of God. By means of the Halacha and Agada, the gifted man trained the layman and shared his finest religious achievements with him.[65]

THE COMMANDMENTS

There are Rabbinic comments concerning the desirability of having many commandments to fulfill. Both Maimonides[66] and Rabbi Joseph Albo (d. 1444)[67] discussed the saying of Rabbi Chanania ben Akashia, "The Holy One, blessed be He, desired to make Israel meritorious, therefore He gave them many laws and commandments."[68] One might think that more laws mean more stumbling blocks and more opportunities for transgressions and punishment. However, both Maimonides and Rabbi Joseph Albo maintained that if a person fulfills even one of the 613 commandments in a proper manner and performs it for its own sake, he thereby merits eternal life. Since every Jew will perform at least one commandment adequately, the rabbis say, "All Israel have a share in the world to come."[69] This, of course, does not exonerate one from performing all of the commandments, as the more commandments a person performs, the closer to perfection he or she comes.

A related question is whether all laws are of equal importance, or is there hierarchy of values within the network of commandments? Rabbi Judah the Prince (HaNassi ca.135–ca.220) admonished, "Be careful to perform a minor commandment just as well as a major one, for you do not know the reward of each commandment."[70] Rabbi Jonah Gerondi (d. 1263) taught that the Torah explained the various penalties and punishments for violations of the negative commandments, such as thirty-nine whip lashings, death and cutting off by Heaven, and the four forms of judicial death penalties. However, the rewards for all of the commandments are not stated in the Torah so that men should perform all of the commandments and not only those that entail greater rewards. He compared all the *mitzvot* to an orchard of trees. If those who planted the various trees knew for which trees they would get paid more, they would plant only the more rewarding ones. However, as all the trees are necessary for the splendor of the orchard, so God wanted to privilege Israel with the fulfillment of all the commandments, which enhance the human personality regardless of the reward attached to performing them.[71]

Not only is there philosophical discussion about the purpose of the Jewish legal system, but there is an exhaustive literature regarding the purpose of individual and groups of commandments and halachot.[72] Some believe that this is a precarious inquiry because one might very well decide not to abide by a particular law if he or she does not agree with the validity of the reasons given for it. Inquiry might result in noncompliance. There is also the view that since the laws are of Divine origin, there is no need to investigate their rationality: The authority of the Lawgiver is sufficient justification for obedience. On the other hand, perhaps one should search for the purpose of the laws *because* they emanate from God. The God-given laws are rational from God's perspective, and one must obey them whether one is able to comprehend their significance or not.

The curiosity of man inevitably led to the investigation of the purpose of the commandments. In addition, Israel's relationship with its neighbors both at home and in exile presented a necessity for the inquiry into the reasons and justifications of the various laws. The Torah itself frequently mentions the purpose inherent in some laws. Two such examples are: (1) The Torah instructs us to set up cities of refuge. Why? So that one who kills unintentionally should flee there from the retaliation of the relatives of the slain.[73] (2) The owner of a field is forbidden by the Torah to reap its edges or to gather the fallen fruits of a vineyard. Why? So that there remains some produce for the poor and the stranger.[74]

Rabbi Saadia Gaon, in explaining the reasons for the commandments, divided them into rational and nonrational ones, the latter being primarily expressions of God's will. He believed that the nonrational commandments have rational aspects and utility, and he repeatedly reminds us of the superiority of God's wisdom over man's.[75] Maimonides rejected this dual distinction of Rabbi Saadia. According to Maimonides, all laws follow from God's wisdom and are not arbitrary acts of His will. He acknowledged that the reason for some commandments is clear while for others it is not; the former fall under the category *mishpatim* and the latter under *chukim*. He interpreted many of the *chukim* as means for abolishing the idolatrous practices of the ancient pagans or for transforming the impure modes of pagan worship to legitimate monotheistic religious Judaism.[76]

Regarding those laws that are usually considered rational by all men (for instance those falling under the domain of ethics), it was the rabbinic opinion that it is preferable to obey them not because they are rational but because it is man's duty to obey the Divine law as promulgated in the Torah. Concerning this the Talmud taught, "He who is commanded and fulfills [the command] is greater than he who fulfills it though not commanded."[77]

We shall conclude this subject with a beautiful comment by Professor Heschel on the topic of the reasons for the *mitzvot*, known in Hebrew as *taamei haMitzvot*. He wrote that the Hebrew word *taam* means taste or flavor, and "It is the flavor that a person perceives in doing a *mitzvah* which communicates its meaning."[78]

ENDNOTES

1. Harold J. Berman, *Talks on American Law* (New York: Vintage, 1961), p. 3.

2. J. J. Roche, "The Net of Law," in *The Pocket Book of Quotations*, ed. Henry Davidoff (New York: Pocket Books, 1955), p. 181.

3. A. Z., 30a.

4. The concept of Jewish law in this chapter refers to the Jewish religious legal system found in the Bible, Talmud, and rabbinic literature, and not to the legal system of the State of Israel or any other Jewish corporate body past or present. Nonetheless, many of the remarks made here are of a general nature and are applicable to these also, and not only to the Halacha.

5. Cited in Aron Barth, *The Modern Jew Faces Eternal Problems*, translated from the Hebrew, By Chaim Schachter (Jerusalem: Religious section of the Youth and HeChalutz Department of the Zionist Organization of America, 1965), p. 22.

6. See the preceding chapter on Jewish Ethics for a discussion of the relation of ethics and law.

7. John Austin, *Lectures on Jurisprudence*, (London: John Murray, 4th ed., 1873), paragraph 60.

8. Ibid., no. 61 and no. 63.

9. Herbert Morris, "Austin, John," in *Encyclopedia of Philosophy*, vol. 1, pp. 209–210.

10. The English legal philosopher H. L. A. Hart, in his *The Concept of Law* (Oxford: Clarendon Press, 1961), rejected the Austinian analysis of law as the sovereign's coercive orders. He understood law in terms of rules.

11. Isadore Twersky, *Introduction to the Code of Maimonides* (New Haven: Yale University Press, 1980), pp. 24–25. See also Maimonides, *Sefer HaMitzvot*, introduction. According to Rabbi Eliyahu Safran, Rabbi Joseph B. Soloveitchik used to say that the *Sefer HaMitzvot* states what the law is, while the *Mishneh Torah* teaches us how to practice the law properly.

12. For information on legal realism, see Yosal Rogat, "Legal Realism," in *Encyclopedia of Philosophy*, vol. 4, pp. 420–421; and M. P. Golding, "Philosophy of Law, Problems of," in *Encyclopedia of Philosophy*, vol. 6, pp. 262–263.

13. Oliver Wendell Holmes, Jr., "The Path of the Law," *Harvard Law Review* 8 (1908), pp. 457–478.

14. Roscoe Pound, "Mechanical Jurisprudence," *Columbia Law Review* 10 (1896), pp. 457–478.

15. Sota 47b.

16. Deut. 30:12.

17. Ex. 23:2.

18. B. M. 59b.

19. R. H. 25b.

20. John Chipman Gray, *The Nature and Sources of the Law* (Boston: Beacon Press, 1909; Citation is from 1963 edition), p. 102.

21. Deut. 16:18. See Midrash Tanchuma on said verse. The observation that both judges and officers are required for the efficacy of a legal system reminds one of President Andrew Jackson's disagreement with the United States Supreme Court, and his remark, "John Marshall made his decision, now let him enforce it."

22. Mishna, San., ch. 1.

23. Harold J. Berman, "Philosophical Aspects of American Law," in Berman, op. cit., pp. 221–222.

24. B. M. 86b.

25. *Shulchan Aruch*, Yoreh Deah 376:4. For a discussion of *minhag* (custom) in Jewish law, see Menachem Elon, "Minhag," in *Encyclopedia Judaica*, vol. 12, pp. 4–26. See also Judah David Eisenstein, *Otzar Dinim Uminhagim* (New York: Hebrew Publishing Co., 1938), pp. 236–237.

26. Milton R. Konvitz, "Savigny, Friedrick Karl von," in *Encyclopedia of Philosophy*, vol. 7, p. 294.

27. Shviit 10:3 and Git. 36a.

28. See the discussion on classification in the chapter on Jewish History.

29. Twersky, op. cit., pp. 274–276 and p. 281, note 92.

30. Meyer Waxman, *A History of Jewish Literature* (New York: Bloch, 1938). See chapters on rabbinic literature, particularly vol. I, pp. 248–250.

31. Salo W. Baron, *A Social and Religious History of the Jews*, 2nd ed., vol. VI (New York: Columbia University and Philadelphia: Jewish Publication Society, 1958), p. 141.

32. C. K. Allen, *Law in the Making* (London: Oxford University Press, 1958: paperback edition, 1961), p. 157.

33. Konvitz, op. cit., p. 294.

34. Boaz Cohen, "The Shulchan Aruch As a Guide for Rabbinical Religious Practice Today," an address at the Rabbinical Assembly Convention, July 5, 1939; published in Boaz Cohen, *Law and Tradition in Judaism* (New York: Jewish Theological Seminary, 1959).

35. Twersky, op. cit., p. 139.

36. Ibid., p. 173.

37. Menachem Elon, "Mishpat Ivri," in *Encyclopedia Judaica*, vol. 12, p. 118.

38. Gray, op. cit., p. 199.

39. Allen, op. cit., pp. 396–408 and Gray, op. cit., pp. 307–309.

40. Cohen, op. cit., p. 194.

41. See the *ViChol Maminim* prayer recited during the Musaf services of Rosh HaShana and Yom Kippur, where it is asserted that God inquires into the most hidden secrets.

42. Shalom Albeck, "Acquisition," in *Encyclopedia Judaica*, vol. 1, p. 217, where it is stated regarding the acquisition of rights that "intention" is required on the part of the acquirer.

43. See the discussion of this subject in the Jewish Ethics chapter.

44. See articles on "Kavana" in *Encyclopedia Judaica*, Eisenstein's *Otzar Dinim Uminhagim*, and Shlomo Zalman Ariel's *Encyclopedia Meir Nativ* (Ramat Gan: Masada, 1968).

45. H. Elchanan Blumenthal, "Kavanah," in *Encyclopedia Judaica*, vol. 10, p. 853.

46. Ibid.

47. Gershom Scholem, *Shabbatai Sevi* (Princeton, NJ: Princeton University Press, 1973), p. 50.

48. Rabbi Joseph B. Soloveitchik, *Halakhic Man* (Philadelphia: Jewish Publication Society, 1983), p. 60–62. This essay originally appeared in Hebrew in 1944 in

the journal *Talpiyot,* vol. 1, nos. 3 and 4. A similar anecdote is related about the Chafetz Chaim (1839–1933). A preacher told the Chafetz Chaim that he arrived in a town where some of its inhabitants were breaking the norms of modesty and purity, and were violating the Sabbath openly. The preacher ascended the pulpit and gave an impassioned sermon about all the town's breaches of sanctity. Before he finished his caustic words, the angry audience forced him off the platform. The Chafetz Chaim asked the downhearted preacher how he delivered his sermon. The preacher replied that he raised his voice at his listeners. The Chafetz Chaim asked the preacher whether he raises his voice with thunder when he puts on *tefillin?* The Chafetz Chaim stated that just as there is no need to rant and thunder when one obeys the commandment of *tefillin,* so there is no need to rant and thunder when one observes the commandment of reproving another person (Vayikra 19:17). See: Moses M. Yoshor, *The Chafetz Chaim: The Life and Works of Rabbi Yisrael Meir Kagan of Radin,* (Brooklyn, New York: Mesorah Publications, Rev. Ed., 1997), p. 312–313.

49. Rabbi Joseph B. Soloveitchik, "Zmanei HaTeshuva ViYichudam," in *Ymei Zikaron* (Jerusalem: Sifriat Eliner SheliYad HaHistadrut HaTzionit HaOlamit, HaMachlaka LiChinuch UliTarbut Torahiyim BaGolah, 1986), p. 236.

50. Isaiah 29:13.

51. Pes. 50b. See also Abraham Joshua Heschel, *Man's Quest for God* (New York: Charles Scribner's Sons, 1954), pp. 96–98.

52. For a description of the James-Lange Theory, see Benjamin B. Wolman, ed., *Handbook of General Psychology* (Englewood Cliffs, NJ: Prentice-Hall, 1973), p. 757. See also Rabbi Moshe Chaim Luzzatto, *The Path of the Just,* English translation by Shraga Silverstein, (Jerusalem and New York: Feldheim, 1966), End of Chapter 7. Luzzatto writes, "For the outer movements cause the inner ones."

53. Abraham J. Heschel, *God in Search of Man* (Philadelphia: Jewish Publication Society, 1955), p. 341.

54. Ibid.

55. Ibid., p. 337.

56. Abraham Holtz, "Kadushin, Max," in *Encyclopedia Judaica,* vol. 10, p. 669.

57. Max Kadushin, *The Rabbinic Mind* (New York: Bloch, 1972), p. 79.

58. Max Kadushin, *Worship and Ethics* (New York: Bloch, 1963), p. 66.

59. Rabbi Joseph B. Soloveitchik, *Halakhic Man,* op. cit., pp. 40–41.

60. Ibid., p. 42.

61. Ibid., pp. 39, 42.

62. Max Kadushin, *Worship and Ethics*, op. cit., p. 178.

63. Max Kadushin, *The Rabbinic Mind*, op. cit., p. 257.

64. Ibid., p. 203.

65. Ibid., pp. 211, 272.

66. Maimonides, Commentary to the Mishna, end of tractate Mak.

67. Rabbi Joseph Albo, *Sefer Ha-Ikkarim*, vol III., trans. by Isaac Husik (Philadelphia: Jewish Publication Society, 1946), pp. 272–278.

68. Mak. 3:16.

69. San. 11:1.

70. Avot 2:1.

71. Rabbi Jonah Gerondi, *The Gates of Repentance*, Gate III, trans. by Shraga Silverstein, (Jerusalem and New York: Feldheim, 1967), chs. 9 and 10. The comparison of the commandments with an orchard of trees is taken from Midrash Tanchuma, Eikev, 2.

72. Much of the material on the subject of the reasons for the commandments is summarized in Yitzchak Heinemann, *Taamei HaMitzvot BiSafrut Yisrael*, 2 vols., (Jerusalem: HaMador HaOati LeInyenei HaNoar ViHeChalutz Shel HaHistadrut HaTzionit, 1954 and 1956). See vol. 1, chs. 1 and 2. See also Alexander Altmann, "Commandments, Reasons for," in *Encyclopedia Judaica*, vol. 5, pp. 783–789.

73. Num. 35:11–12; Deut. 19:4–7.

74. Lev. 19:9.

75. Rabbi Saadia Gaon, *Book of Beliefs and Opinions*, Treatise 3.

76. Maimonides, *Guide for the Perplexed*, Part 3.

77. Kid. 31a; B. K. 38a; B. K. 87a. There is a discussion on this subject in the Jewish Ethics chapter.

78. Heschel, *God in Search of Man*, op. cit., p. 354.

FIVE

JEWISH EDUCATION

I t is well known that education plays a paramount role in Jewish society. For instance, it is debated in the Talmud who is to be given precedence   in certain matters, one's father or one's teacher?[1] There is a rabbinic discussion about what is greater, study or deeds? The answer that was proposed is that study is more important because it leads to deeds.[2] We are informed by Hillel that "An empty-headed person cannot be sin-fearing, nor can an ignorant one be pious."[3] There is no question about it: Jews accentuate and love learning.

Besides the usual value people place on education, it has an even more profound political and theological significance in Jewish life. Plato, in his *Republic*, described the ideal state, as existing only when "Philosophers are kings, or the kings of this world have the spirit and power of philosophy."[4] Rabbi Joseph B. Soloveitchik pointed out that in Judaism the ideal leaders of the people are the teachers. Moses is referred to as *Moshe Rabbeinu*, (Moses, our teacher) and not as King Moses. He cited *Gittin* 62a, where it is written that rabbis are called kings.[5]

Rabbis and teachers have held positions of leadership and power throughout Jewish history, and they have been respected and admired by the Jewish populace. The Jewish people have almost always revered the wise teacher—not only for his wisdom, erudition, and teaching, but also for the ethical integrity that is a part of his personal life.

As would be expected, philosophers have taken a keen interest in education. This is not surprising, as both philosophy and education are concerned with knowledge and wisdom. Much of what philosophers have to say regarding education in general is also applicable to Jewish education.

The philosophy of education deals with problems such as these: What are the major goals of education? What are the most important subjects to be taught and at what age level? How should the school program be organized? What are the best teaching methods? Should schools attempt to educate all children equally? Should schools be child-centered, or subject-centered, or perhaps society-centered? How should teachers be trained? How is education related to such disciplines as psychology and theories of learning?[6]

The philosophy of education also has an analytical and critical side. It asks: What is education? What constitutes an educated person? What is meant by such educational terms as academic freedom, adjustment, democracy in the classroom, experience, growth, etc.?

Education is frequently divided into two categories, one formal and technical, the other informal and broad. The first type is usually acquired through institutions of learning and might include such things as knowledge of the Bible and its commentaries, the study of Talmud, and Jewish history. The latter type of education is procured by experience from people or groups whose primary purpose is not organized education, and might include the proper way to put on *tefillin* or how to conduct a prayer service in the synagogue.

Education is sometimes considered a product and sometimes a process. *What* we have learned is a product of education; *how* we learned it is the process of education.[7]

GOALS OF JEWISH EDUCATION

A major problem in the philosophy of education is determining the goals of education. This problem naturally is closely related to one's general outlook and *weltanschauung*. A Zionist school, for instance, has different goals from a yeshiva, and both differ from a Yiddishist school. The goals of a Zionist oriented school are usually tilted toward the national, and often secular, nature of the Jewish people, with an emphasis on the Hebrew language and Hebrew literature. The yeshiva aims at educating pupils to continue the practice of Judaism through the traditional intensive study of the Talmud and rabbinic literature. Yiddishist schools seek to disseminate the richness of the Yiddish language and culture that flourished among East European Jewry before the Holocaust.

What qualities does a person need to possess in order to be educated? Is it necessary to have acquired 120 college credits, and is one necessarily well-educated if he or she possesses them? Is a well-read layman with little formal schooling an educated person? Is having a good vocabulary with superior language and communication skills a necessary condition of being considered well-educated? What if someone is an expert in chemistry but knows little about the arts and humanities, or vice versa: is he or she an educated person? Does a person have the required credentials if he or she has all the academic qualities in the world but is lacking common sense, the so-called fifth *Shulchan Aruch*? What if someone is a walking encyclopedia but his or her critical thinking is suffering a crisis? And even if one possesses all the usual qualifications, what happens if that person's learning "goes to his head," if his or her character is blemished, or if he or she remains a *schlemieh*? Is it usually possible to spot an educated individual in his or her everyday existence or ordinary conversation,[8] or are there concealed scholars just as there are hidden saints?[9]

One cannot enumerate with precision all the necessary and sufficient requirements for being educated. However, having in mind what the requisites are—even if only in a general manner—is a helpful guide to the educator. It indicates the kind of person he or she is trying to mold or influence and consequently facilitates the determination of what is to be taught, and in general is helpful for the process of education.

WHO IS AN EDUCATED JEW?

We are now approaching the intriguing question of what constitutes an educated Jewish person. There probably will be more controversy in this area than that concerning general education. There will be as many different views as there are different Jews.

Most educators would require that a person with a good Jewish education should have a solid knowledge of the entire Bible or major parts of it though, most *yeshivot* would not. Many schools would require just a modicum of knowledge of the Talmud, whereas *yeshivot* and many day schools make the Talmud the main or almost exclusive requirement of satisfactory Jewish education. Even within the area of talmudic education itself, there is disagreement whether students should cover much textual material or concentrate more intensively on less material, perhaps even with casuistry. It also needs to be considered which sections of the Talmud should be studied, since the entire six divisions of the text are not covered in the classroom because of its vast material.

What is the role of language instruction in the Jewish school? Should the primary language be Hebrew, Yiddish, or English? Since English is the mother tongue in the United States and is understood by all students, should instruction take place mainly or exclusively in that idiom? Since Yiddish plays a very prominent role in the Ashkenazic European culture that is a great part of the Jewish heritage, perhaps that vernacular should be stressed in a Jewish school? In the advanced grades of many *yeshivot*, there are rabbis who teach in Yiddish, and therefore many deans of *yeshivot* and Orthodox Jewish day schools feel that it is a necessity for their pupils to at least comprehend spoken Yiddish and have some ability to converse in that tongue.

Hebrew, of course, is the official language in the Land of Israel and is the language of the Bible and a great part of Jewish literature. It would appear that the Hebrew language should certainly be a major part of the curriculum of any Jewish school. The question is how much Hebrew should be taught? Should it be required to a conversational level or only a reading knowledge? Should Hebrew be a special, individual subject, or should it simply be taught while studying and translating the Bible? What about Hebrew grammar? Should it be part of the curriculum—and if yes, at what grade level?

The connection between language and knowledge is an interesting philosophical inquiry. Would there be knowledge at all if there were not language? Certainly it would be of a very primitive sort. Are people able to think if they use no words? If we are unable to put our thoughts into words, is that a sure sign that our thoughts are not clear even to ourselves? Certainly the communication of our thoughts to others requires language skills. Do sloppy language habits imply slovenly thinking? Is a good vocabulary a component of a good education, or merely a sign of one? These questions about the role and importance of language for education should be considered by Jewish educators. A proper answer to them might have more than mere theoretical import.

Is Jewish history a necessary ingredient of the Jewish educational experience? Although the Bible is replete with historical writing, it was not until recent times that much history was written by Jews in comparison with their entire literary output. Since Josephus wrote *The Antiquities of the Jews* in 93 C.E., no comprehensive history of the Jewish people was composed by a Jew until the nineteenth century.[10] For medieval Judaism, "Historiography never became a legitimate and recognized genre."[11] The historical works that were written often contained apologetic introductions, and were usually read more for purposes of leisure and moral uplift than for serious scholarship.[12] Studying history was relegated to the category of *Bittul Torah*, with time better spent perusing religious texts.[13]

Historical inquiry was maligned within the rabbinic field of study itself. It is related that a Talmudic sage was repudiated by a "modern" scholar because he was not acquainted even with the history of the talmudic age and the history of rabbinic studies. The sage replied that if someone wants to know what kind of tobacco the Rambam (Maimonides) utilized, he will inquire of the modern scholar with historical training; however, one who desires to know the contents of what the Rambam taught will approach the old style talmudic student or rabbinic scholar.

Despite these remarks, most (but not all) Jewish schools do require that their pupils study at least some Jewish history. After all, a people without knowledge of its history is analogous to a person walking the streets while suffering amnesia.

What about other areas of Jewish culture? Should the educated person be acquainted with Jewish philosophy, mysticism, art, literature, and music? How much time, if any, of the school day should be devoted to these Jewish fields?

Just as the educator's goals are largely determined by his or her general and Jewish philosophical outlook, so these views also influence his conception of what is meant by a well-educated person. They help him or her decide what subjects the school should teach in order to deliver a quality education.

Different goals naturally call for different curricula. Nevertheless, there should be some common ground within Jewish schools despite their differences. At least some Bible, Talmud, and Jewish history should be required study as part of the heritage that all Jews share in common.

Another important question in general education, and also in Jewish education, is whether the school is doing its job if it does not instill ethical behavior and values within the student body? In the Jewish school, intellectual development is supposed to be paralleled by ethical growth. Not only do Jewish teachings strive for moral perfection, the Jewish teacher is expected to set the prime example. To this day, the biographies of Torah scholars, teachers, and hasidic masters are studied not necessarily to understand their teachings or for historical purposes, but rather to derive inspiration from their pious and saintly behavior. It is part of hasidic lore that Rabbi Leib the Son of Sarah visited the Mezheritzer Magid, Rabbi Dov Ber (ca. 1710–1772), not to learn Torah interpretations from him, but to see how he put on his shoes and tied his shoelaces.[14] On Simchat Torah, Jews dance with the Torah and frequently sing, "*Moshe Emet, ViTorato Emet*," (Moses is True and so also is his Torah).[15]

There is no doubt that ethics is an essential part of the Jewish religion. A controversy arose concerning how it should be incorporated into the educational system. Rabbi Isaac Blaser (1837–1907) wanted to introduce the study of *musar* (ethics) into the yeshiva of Volozhin. Rabbi

Chaim Soloveitchik (1853–1918) opposed by saying that *musar* is like a medicine for the spiritually ill. Students who study Torah are healthy and do not require such special medication.[16] Eventually many *yeshivot* did introduce *musar* as part of the study program, usually under the direction of special instructors, known as *mashgichim*, who had great influence upon the character development of their students. At any rate, all agree that ethical conduct should result from Jewish education.

Another issue is to what extent, if any, should secular studies be part of a Jewish education? There are those who believe that some secular studies are required in order to understand certain aspects of Jewish studies, including areas within rabbinic literature, such as the calculation of the new moon and matters of the Jewish calender upon which the festivals depend. This attitude, among others, is associated with the Vilna Gaon.[17] Most members of the right wing Orthodox movement believe vehemently that secular studies have no place at all in the education of a loyal Jew, especially a Jewish male, and should be shunned. Others maintain that a person well educated in Judaica should also have a good secular education, which reflects the high intellectual achievements of mankind. One's general philosophy, again, will determine one's attitude on this issue.[18]

Even though there are differences of opinion about what an educated person should know, most would agree that he should not be a "parrot" scholar; rather he should be capable of critical thinking. Probably the greatest critical thinking taught and practiced in any school takes place at *yeshivot*, even in early grades of study and certainly at advanced levels. The essence of the talmudic dialectic involves intellectual acumen. However, it is interesting that most *yeshivot* oppose introducing their students to general or Jewish philosophy. There is fear that critical thinking outside the talmudic realm or about talmudic civilization might lead to unhealthy skepticism, or at the least detracts from time and energy expended solely on rabbinics. Free thought within the system is of its essence, but it must remain within its own parameters.

It is recognized that a good deal of education involves repetition of what one reads in books or hears from teachers, and repetition often involves word-for-word memorization. Knowing the subject matter is, of course, essential, but too much stress on this type of learning does hinder creative thinking. Which is more important: book learning, critical thinking, or creative originality? Who is greater: the walking encyclopedia, referred to in the Talmud as "Sinai," or the sharp thinker who could pass an elephant through the eye of a needle, the so-called "Uprooter of Mountains?"[19] Is creativity possible without any book knowledge, or only a modicum of it?

In a 1978 Chanukah *maamar*, or lecture, Rabbi Yitzchok Hutner inquired about the logical consistency of two requests made by the worshipper during the daily morning prayers: (1) "Make the words of Thy Torah sweet in our mouth" ("*Vihaarev na*") and (2) "Make Thy Torah a habit with us" ("*Shetargileinu BiTorahtecha*"). If the Torah learning is to be sweet, how could it be like a routine habit; and if it is habitual and rote-like, how could it be sweet? Rabbi Hutner explained that the educational process first requires basic knowledge that the student must master thoroughly, so that it becomes a part of his or her very being— like, for instance, one knows the letters of the alphabet. Then the student proceeds to advance and build upon such rote knowledge, which constitutes the sweetness of learning. This new knowledge itself subsequently becomes second nature to the student, and he or she then creates and experiences new learning based upon it. Thus, the path of education combines both rote learning and sweetness of learning in a dialectical process, where one builds and creates upon the the other in a continuous fashion.[20]

It is difficult for the educator to determine what is the proper balance or how much weight should be given to book knowledge, critical thinking, and original thinking. A partial solution to this question involves giving consideration to the variegated aptitudes and interests of the students themselves. Pupils endowed with good memories should be encouraged toward information-gathering learning. Those with sharp minds should be directed toward areas where critical thinking is paramount. Students with a creative inclination should receive encouragement to enhance their originality. This is not to imply that the student should decide what kind of an education he or she should receive. It does mean that the student should be encouraged in those areas in which he or she excels.

It is interesting that the traditional *yeshivot,* perhaps more so than more progressive educational institutions, adjust the talmudic course of study to accord with the different aptitudes of their student bodies. They encourage study that covers much textual material, critical thinking, and cultivation of originality of thought. Just about every advanced yeshiva has some students who absorb vast quantities of the talmudic text plus cognate branches of rabbinic literature, and perhaps even memorize a large portion of the Talmud. The question and answer method of the Talmud itself and of yeshiva instruction prompts students to think for themselves and to think critically. The dialectical method of talmudic study involves the students in questioning what they learn, to ferret out difficulties and contradictions. This frequently culminates with students themselves offering solutions and original interpretations and expressing themselves in a creative manner.

The development of their students' minds in and through rabbinic studies is a major achievement of the Yeshiva system. However, it does not provide adequately for those students who are incapable of following talmudic discourse, or for those whose interests lie in different areas of study, even within the field of Jewish scholarship.

Parenthetically, when dealing with the education and aptitudes of children, it should be kept in mind that the word children includes boys and girls. Both girls and boys are discriminated against, to everyone's detriment, when important areas of Jewish learning are deliberately withheld from them.[21]

An interesting question in educational theory relevant to Jewish pedagogy is whether the school should center around society, the child, or subject matter? Whenever a society organizes a school or institutions of learning, it wants to bequeath to the next generation the best and most noble accomplishments of the human past and its highest aspirations for the future. To a large extent the values of society form the nucleus of an educational system.

In Jewish life, particularly in the Diaspora, there is a legitimate concern and apprehension that without the Jewish school, the younger generation would entirely assimilate within society at large and Judaism and Jewish civilization would eventually disappear—or certainly diminish greatly. Jewish education is equated with Jewish survival. If the tradition is not handed over in *yeshivot*, day schools, and congregational schools, the fear is that there will be no tradition left in the future. Thus, within Jewish education it seems correct to say that the school is society-oriented, perhaps moreso than in most educational systems.

Still, even within the society-centered Jewish school the child is not simply like clay in the hands of the societal potter. There are limitations on how much children can and should be molded. No two children are identical. There is a variety in the learning abilities and needs of each child. The slow learner cannot have the learning material heaped upon him in the same manner as the gifted child. Even within the so-called range of normalcy, there are infinite differences among students.

There is no educator, including the Jewish one, who does not wrestle with the problem of the most appropriate way to place children in parallel classes. Should these classes be divided according to a homogeneous or heterogeneous grouping? Should gifted or slow children be separated in different classrooms from average learners? If they are not separated, does this signify that the school is not presenting the best educational environment for the gifted to develop their full potential, which may be of great benefit for the rest of society? Obviously, the needs of the children themselves have to be considered along with the noble wishes of society at large.

EDUCATIONAL THEORIES AND JEWISH EDUCATION

Society wishes to reach out to the next generation. The road to the future is education, and the main highway is subject matter. It has already been stated that the goals of the educator and the needs of the student interact in determining what subjects will be taught and which will be stressed.

It is obvious that much subject mater is communicated through the medium of books, the written word. Frequently, whether properly or not, education is equated with book learning. Jewish civilization puts a premium upon books, starting with the Bible. Jews are referred to as the People of the Book.[22] There are many outstanding books with Jewish content that have been written throughout history. Many of these can properly be called classics, but it is amazing how few of them, and other excellent writings, are required reading in Jewish schools, even at the highest levels of Jewish education.[23] There is no advocating here for a "Great Books" program such as is associated with the Perrenialism theory of education advocated by Robert M. Hutchins and Mortimer J. Adler.[24] However, a more extensive familiarity with great Jewish books should be a desideratum within Jewish education. Perhaps some of them should be required summer reading in the higher grade levels?

The end of the nineteenth century saw the birth of the Progressive Education movement. It was a rebellion against "the excessive formalism of traditional education with its emphasis on strict discipline, passive learning, and pointless drill,"[25] and is associated with such people as John Dewey and William H. Kilpatrick of Columbia University, among others. Since the Soviet Union launched its Sputnik into outer space in 1957, Progressive Education has fallen into disfavor. It has been blamed for the decline in the standards of education and the deterioration of the knowledge of reading, writing, and arithmetic. While Progressivism undoubtedly went too far, it does have some valid pedagogical ideas that could and should be applied within the schools, including Jewish schools.

The Progressive idea of relating subject matter to the interests of the child, when applied intelligently, can be a great stimulus to meaningful learning. This does not at all imply that the child should be taught only what interests him or her. However, one does learn better and remembers more if what he learns interests him. A good teacher motivates a student so that the student likes what he learns, even if he does not always learn what he likes.

The educational theory known as Essentialism[26] correctly requires that there must be a set curriculum, that the child cannot make the decisions about the content of his or her education. A child lacks the knowledge and experience to be a philosopher of education or a professional educator and cannot decide what subjects are essential for life when he or she has hardly begun to live himself or herself. This does not mean that a person's education should or must be stuffed down his throat or into his brain. The subject matter to be taught should be sweetened as much as possible through proper motivation. Where applicable, rewards can make learning an enticing experience just as an appealing topping makes a cake irresistible.

The Progressive ideas of experiential learning, learning through doing, and the project method can be applied profitably to Jewish education. Here are some examples: (1) having a model seder; (2) visiting a Jewish exhibit or museum; (3) touring a matzah bakery; (4) presenting audiovisual aids, such as a slide program illustrating the thirty-nine categories of work forbidden on the Sabbath; and (5) spending some time in a Jewish library, which would enable students to acquire hands-on experience with Jewish reference books. Arts and crafts and music should be brought into Jewish learning, at least occasionally, to make it more alive and inviting. Individual or groups could work on a scholarly assignment and report their results to the rest of the class. This type of project learning is valuable socially, for the experience of doing research utilizing Jewish books and periodicals, and for developing verbal skills in presenting one's findings in a public classroom.

Some teachers use Progressive methods better than others. To what extent they should be utilized in the schoolhouse is difficult to determine with precision. However, they should not be overdone or utilized exclusively. After all, the teacher, an educated and professionally trained adult, should know more and be better able to teach than the students who report to the class the results of their own or group research. Presumably, whether education is free or tuition is charged, parents hope and expect that their children learn primarily from their teachers rather than from their peers.

When we think of education, we usually think mainly of students, for it is for them that the educational system exists. However, an important and perhaps vital question is determining the best way to train teachers. Are good teachers made or born? Is teaching a science or an art? How much academic subject matter should the teacher be required to master, especially if he or she is teaching in the lower grades? How many and what kind of education courses should be taught to the prospective teacher? What proportion of these courses should be devoted to educational theory, history, and methods? How much instruction should he or she receive in the area of psychology? All these questions have theoretical and practical significance when considering how to provide better teachers within the fold of Jewish education.

Jewish education can learn much from the problems presented and solutions offered by educational psychology. How do children (and adults) learn? What is the optimum amount of review that is required for retention? The Talmud asserts that "The one who learns his lesson a hundred times is not to be compared with him who learns it one hundred and one times." [27] Is this assertion valid for all areas of study or only for some types of subject matter? Does constant review for some reach a point of diminishing returns? Excessive review, together with its unpopular cousin, constant drill, can lead to boredom and have a negative impact upon learning.

Are there particular hours of the day when there is more productivity in learning? If there are, these times should be used to their maximum. Some people are more alert during the morning hours, whereas others are more efficient at other times. Many people feel that they remember best the following day that which they review or memorize shortly before retiring for the night. There are a number of mnemonic devices that can aid the student. Teachers should utilize them and inform their students regarding them.

It is generally accepted that one learns best and with the least amount of exertion during one's youth. Elisha ben Avuya said, "If one learns when he is young, to what is he like? To ink written on new paper. If one learns when he is old, to what is he like? To ink written on blotted paper." [28] It is also generally accepted that various subjects are best taught during certain developmental stages of a person's growth. Thus, young children have a greater facility for learning languages. While theoretical physics and higher mathematics can best be postponed for a later stage of an individual's development.[29] This theory of learning readiness was already mentioned by Rabbi Judah ben Tema in the middle of the second century: "At five years the age is reached for the study of the Bible, at ten for the study of Mishna, at thirteen for the fulfillment of the commandments, at fifteen for the study of Talmud."[30]

Educators have much to learn from the field of industrial psychology. Studies indicate that in the work place, employees perform better under favorable environmental conditions such as proper lighting, periodic recess breaks to reduce fatigue, task rotation to minimize monotony and boredom, opportunity to participate in the decision-making process, and having management periodically explain the logic of its operation.[31] Just as time-and-motion study[32] is used in industrial management in order to increase operating efficiency, so its equivalent should be utilized to increase productivity within general and Jewish education. There is need for education management just as there is need for industrial management, and it is just as important.

It unquestionably is recognized that there are many teachers who do a good job even without taking education courses. Frequently the education department of a college or seminary is not among the most respected on the campus. But let this not be taken to mean that education courses, such as the philosophy of education and of Jewish education, are insignificant chatter. Every Jewish teacher does a better job if he or she is equipped with a general Jewish philosophy and with a philosophy of Jewish education. Professor George F. Kneller succinctly summarized the significance of our subject with these words: "An educator who does not use philosophy is inevitably superficial. A superficial educator may be good or bad—but if good, less good than he could be, and if bad, worse than he need be."[33]

ENDNOTES

1. B. M. 33a.

2. Kid. 40b.

3. Avot 2:6.

4. Plato, *Republic*, book V, 473.

5. Rabbi Joseph B. Soloveitchik, "Who is Fit to Lead the Jewish People?" in Abraham R. Besdin, ed., *Reflections of the Rav* (Jerusalem: Department for Torah Education and Culture in the Diaspora of the World Zionist Organization, 1979), pp. 127–138. It is interesting to note that Rabbi Akiva advised his son not to reside in a city whose leaders are scholars (Pes. 112).

6. R. Freeman Butts, "Education," in *World Book Encyclopedia*, 1972.

7. George F. Kneller, *Introduction to the Philosophy of Education* (New York: John Wiley & Sons, 1964), p. 21.

8. "Even the ordinary conversation (*sichat chulin*) of a scholar requires study." See A. Z. 19b, and Suk. 21b.

9. The analogy is to the "thirty-six hidden saints" in each generation in whose merits the rest of the populace is sustained. See article "Lamed Vav Zadikim," in *Encyclopedia Judaica*, vol. 10, pp. 1367–1368. See also Gershom Scholem, "The Tradition of the Thirty-Six Hidden Just Men," in his *The Messianic Idea in Judaism* (New York: Schocken, 1971), pp. 251–256.

10. Cecil Roth, "Historiography," in *Encyclopedia Judaica*, vol. 8., pp. 560–562.

11. Yosef Hayim Yerushalmi, *Zakhor* (Philadelphia: Jewish Publication Society and Seattle: University of Washington Press, 1982), p. 66.

12. Ibid., pp. 66–69.

13. Rabbi Yitzchok Hutner wrote that it is an error to believe that Jews did not study history because it involves taking time away from Torah study or because it is a waste of time. He identified Israel with the Torah ("Israel and the Torah are one." See *Zohar*, Acharei). A proper understanding of the Torah requires the exegesis of Rashi and other commentators. Since no such commentaries exist for a proper understanding of Jewish history, it cannot be studied adequately. See: Rabbi Yitzchok Hutner, *Pachad Yitzchak: Igrot Uchtavim* (Jerusalem: HaMosad Gur Aryeh, 1971), Letter no. 86, p. 162.

14. Martin Buber, *Tales of the Hasidim*, vol. I (New York: Schocken, 1961), p. 107; Louis J. Newman and Samuel Spitz, eds., *The Hasidic Anthology* (New York: Bloch, 1944), pp. 29–30.

15. B. B. 74a.

16. Rabbi Joseph B. Soloveitchik, *Halakhic Man* (Philadelphia: Jewish Publication Society, 1983), pp. 74–76; Rabbi Dov Katz, *Pulmus HaMusar* (Jerusalem: (No Publisher) 1972), pp. 292–294.

17. See articles on the Vilna Gaon by Rabbi Samuel K. Mirsky in *Encyclopedia Judaica*, vol. 6, p. 655 and M. M. Yoshor, "Eliyahu of Vilna," in *Jewish Leaders*, ed. Leo Jung (Jerusalem: Boys Town, 1964), p. 33.

18. On the role of secular studies in relation to Jewish education, see Rabbi Moshe Weinberger, "On Studying Secular Subjects," *Journal of Halacha and Contemporary Society*, XI (Spring 1986) pp. 88–128. The article cites the literature pertaining to the subject.

19. It is recorded that the students of the Babylonian Yeshiva of Pumbedita, founded by Rabbi Judah ben Ezekiel (d. 299), were renowned for the sharpness of their minds, that they were able to "pass an elephant through the eye of a needle." See B. M. 38b. The expressions, "Sinai" and "Okeir Harim" or "Uprooter of Mountains" refer respectively to Rabbi Joseph, who had a vast knowledge of the tradition, and Rabbah, who possessed exceptional dialectical skill. These two scholars were under consideration to head the Pumbedita academy after the death of Rabbi Judah ben Ezekiel. The question was asked of the Palestinian scholars: Who should be given preference, "Sinai" or the "Uprooter of Mountains?" They cast their vote for "Sinai." However, Rabbi Joseph did not accept the position, which went to Rabbah. After Rabbah's death, twenty-two years afterwards, Rabbi Joseph succeeded him for two and a half years. See Ber. 64a.

20. I am indebted to my nephew for making the tape of Rabbi Hutner's *maamar* available to me.

21. For a brief discussion of the status of girls and women in Jewish education, see Joel B. Wolowelsky, *Women, Jewish Law, and Modernity* (Hoboken, NJ: Ktav, 1997), pp. 111–118. The approval of Rabbi Joseph B. Soloveitchik for women studying Talmud is evident from a class for women he conducted on that subject at Stern College. His son-in-law, Rabbi Aharon Lichtenstein, wrote that he has no objection to teaching girls Talmud, especially that they should have the ability to learn, understand, and enjoy a page of Talmud.

22. The expression "People of the Book" was perhaps first found in Sura III of the Koran, and has had various interpretations. Cecil Roth understood the phrase to mean, among other things, that the Jews are a literary people who, to an unusual extent, have been interested in books. See Cecil Roth, "The Jewish Love of Books," in *Essays on Jewish Booklore* Edited by Philip Goodman (New York: Ktav and Jewish Book Council) 1972, pp. 179–184. See also Ludwig Lewisohn, "The Jew and the Book," in Samuel Caplan and Harold Ribalow, eds., *The Great Jewish Books* (New York: Washington Square Press, 1963), pp. 13–28.

23. There is no intent here of citing specific titles of Jewish classics, only to point out the neglect of so many of them by Jewish schools.

24. For a discussion of Perrenialism as an educational theory, see Kneller, op. cit., pp. 108–113.

25. Kneller, op. cit., p. 94. For a discussion of the theories of Progressive Education, see Kneller, pp. 94–107.

26. Ibid., pp. 113–119 for a discussion of Essentialism.

27. Chag. 9b.

28. Avot 4:25.

29. Developmental psychology is associated with such people as Arnold Gessell, Jean Piaget, and Erik Erikson.

30. Avot 5:24.

31. The 1927 Hawthorne Studies in the area of industrial management centered around working conditions and the environmental approach to increase productivity.

32. Frederick W. Taylor (1856–1915) pioneered time-and-motion study.

33. Kneller, op. cit., p. 128.

SIX

JEWISH THEOLOGY

The philosophy of religion, like that of law, science, or art, is a branch of philosophy. However, since both philosophy and religion deal with ultimate questions, it is sometimes difficult to draw the line of demarcation between them. When philosophy serves the needs of religion with the goal of justifying it, the philosophical activity is usually referred to as natural theology. When it examines religion in a nonpartisan manner with no agenda to serve, then it falls under the category of philosophy. In practice, philosophy of religion historically has been an amalgam of both types of thinking.[1]

Instructive regarding our subject is the statement of Anselm of Canterbury: "For I do not seek to understand that I may believe, but I believe in order to understand. For this I also believe—that unless I believed, I should not understand."[2] This is the view not of a naive believer, but of a rationalist who firmly opposed the anti-intellectualism of his day,[3] and whose name is associated with the famed ontological argument for the existence of God. In a somewhat analogous Jewish version, the Biblical phrase *Naaseh ViNishma*, "We shall do and we shall hear [or understand],"[4] can be interpreted to mean that performing commandments precedes and leads to insight and understanding.

In modern times, we like to believe that philosophy takes no sides and examines all issues, including religion, without preconceptions. We want first to understand, and only afterwards, if conditions and conclusions warrant, are we willing to believe and to practice. Professor Emil L. Fackenheim questioned whether modern philosophy actually is universal, whether it is impartial, and whether it is neither Jewish nor Christian? He concluded by responding in the negative, writing that in a Christian world, modern philosophy is "guilty of an unconscious parochialism contrary to its own conscious aspirations." [5]

The philosophy of religion subjects the claims of religion to rational criticism and investigates the logic of religious discourse. It is largely occupied with reasons for or against various fundamental religious beliefs, especially the belief in God.[6] It asks such questions as: What is meant by religion? What is the nature of religious experience? How do faith and reason relate to each other? Can God's existence be proven? What are the basic tenets of religion and are they rationally tenable? What is the relationship between religion and ethics and between religion and science? How does religion view man and what does it demand of him?

JUDAISM

If one were to examine the many definitions that have been offered for religion, one would be unable to find an all-encompassing one.[7] For purposes of this book, we are concerned about the definition or at least the underlying character or qualities of the Jewish religion, or Judaism. We can ask two basic questions in this regard: (1) What is the essence of present-day Judaism, and (2) is the core of contemporary Judaism the same as medieval, talmudic, or even biblical Judaism? Would Maimonides recognize the *Baal Shem Tov* and how do they relate to Jeremiah, Rabbi Akiva, or to the Jewish world we live in?

In the Philosophy of Law chapter, we quoted Professor Zalman B. Rabinkoff to the effect that Halacha was the binding agent that enabled Judaism to survive intact despite the diversification within of ideologies and sects throughout the ages.[8] Halacha played a dominant role in the life of each Jew, learned and simple-minded alike. Today, even among the reform Jews, as well as among the so-called "unobservant Orthodox," *mitzvot* are constantly being performed, whether at a Passover Seder, during a High Holy Day service, in times of gladness or sadness, or when one gives charity to a Jewish cause, etc. All Jews, even with minimal adherence to their religion, "even the emptiest among them [lit. you] are as full of meritorious deeds as a pomegranate [of seeds]," in the words of the third century rabbi, Resh Lakish.[9] Halacha undoubtedly is an essential component of Judaism, and an undeniable one. Those who tamper with it flippantly present a clear and present danger to Judaism.

In connection with the topic of Halacha, we can find a partial answer to how different ages and places of Judaism relate to each other. Rabbi Joseph B. Soloveitchik presented us with the following scenario: We enter a classroom where students study Talmud or Halacha, and there we are able to discover the contemporaneity of all ages of Judaism. Students argue a point of law and quote different rabbinic sages who lived throughout Jewish history as if they all were concurrently present, discussing and arguing with each other at one given moment and in one given place.[10] In this schoolroom context there exists a Jewish line of communication that extends from ancient times to the present time.

Halacha represents Judaism in practice, but there is also Judaism in thought. Although there has been less uniformity of Jewish thinking compared with Jewish living, Judaism does have an ideational component alongside its behavioral one. Various attempts have been made to summarize the principles of Jewish faith, the most famous being Maimonides' "Thirteen Principles of Faith," which are: (1) there is a Creator, (2) He is one, (3) He is incorporeal, (4) He is eternal, (5) He alone must be worshiped, (6) the Prophets are true, (7) Moses was the greatest prophet, (8) the entire Torah was given by God to Moses, (9) the Torah is immutable, (10) God knows all human acts and thoughts, (11) He rewards and punishes, (12) the Messiah will come, and (13) resurrection of the dead will take place.[11] Rabbis Chasdai Crescas (d. 1410?), Simon ben Tzemach Duran (1361–1444), and Joseph Albo (ca. 1380–ca.1435) proposed different beliefs that are essential to Judaism, with the latter two reducing the cardinal beliefs to: (1) existence of God, (2) revelation, and (3) reward and punishment. It should not be interpreted that these three principles of belief constitute the entire spectrum of the Jewish intellectual outlook. Rabbi Albo, for instance, derived "roots" from his three fundamental principles that are equally obligatory upon the adherent to the Jewish religion. On the other hand, Don Isaac Abarbanel (1437–1508) in his *Rosh Amana* maintained that no purpose is served by establishing cardinal beliefs of Judaism. In spite of this, the Abarbanel could not resist the temptation and wrote that if he were to select one basic principle of the Torah, it would be that the world was created.[12]

Mention should be made that there have also been attempts at reducing the Halacha to basic principles. The 613 commandments were reduced by King David to eleven, by Isaiah to six, by Micah to three, and by Chabakuk to one principle: "But the righteous shall live by his faith."[13] The Ten Commandments, according to some, have also served as all-inclusive principles containing the rest of the commandments within them.[14]

When considering the nature of the Jewish religion, it is useful to bear in mind that Judaism is a trifocal religion. It focuses in three directions simultaneously. First, it zooms in on personal perfection and salvation, confirmed by the fact that many of the Biblical commandments are articulated in the second person singular. It also widens its purview toward a universal Messianic utopia where all people live in peace and harmony. At the same time, Judaism concentrates on the midrange of the spectrum by advocating a national role for the Jewish people within the family of mankind.

JUDAISM AND GOD

The problems addressed by the philosophy of religion vary from one religion to another. The problems of main interest to a Hindu or Buddhist are different from those that occupy a philosopher of Judaism or of its daughter religions.[15] A cornerstone of the philosophy of Judaism is justifying belief or faith in God and trying to portray His attributes, to prove God's existence and to delineate His qualities, to show that He is and describe what He is.

Early medieval Jewish philosophers like Rabbis Saadia Gaon, Bachya Ibn Pakuda and Joseph Ibn Zadik (d. 1149), following the method of the Arabic Kalam, proved the existence of God by first showing that the universe was created, and hence it follows that a Creator exists. Maimonides rejected the method of proving God's existence as a corollary of the creation of the world. He tried to show that God exists even if matter were eternal, as was the common Aristotelian and medieval view, and used cosmological proofs for God's existence. For instance, there is motion in the world that is caused by previous motion, a process that cannot go back infinitely and must culminate in a first unmoved mover who is the ultimate cause of all motion. This unmoved mover is God. Maimonides also taught that all contingent existence is ultimately dependent upon a necessary existent, who is God. Gersonides (1288–1344) resorted to the teleological proof of God's existence: Since the celestial and terrestial worlds constitute an orderly, unitary whole, they point to a Supreme Being who produces and knows this order.[16]

Since Immanuel Kant cast doubt upon the logical validity of the classical proofs of God's existence within the realm of pure reason, offering such proofs has fallen out of favor. It should, however, be accentuated here that there also is no way that reason can disprove God's existence.[17] Another serious objection to the philosophical proofs of God's existence is that the God so proven to exist is not the God most people worship. The religious person, in Pascal's words, craves for the "God of Abraham, God of Isaac, God of Jacob, not of the philosophers and scholars."[18] Pascal's words are similar to the view of Rabbi Judah Halevi (d. 1141), who argued that philosophy reduces God to an impersonal force, one not concerned about people and their prayers. Although not negating philosophical activity, Halevi based his belief in God mainly on the existence of the Jewish nation and its remarkable history. God revealed Himself at Mount Sinai in the presence of the entire people who themselves attest to the authenticity of the revelation.[19] Halevi had an empirical approach to understanding Judaism and did not find it necessary to prove God's existence in the traditional scholastic manner of medieval philosophy.

With the logical difficulties of presenting rational proofs for the existence of God, post-Kantian thinkers resorted to an experiential approach to vindicate the legitimacy and intellectual respectability of religion. Examples of this type of thinking by Jewish philosophers are found in the existentialist thought of Franz Rosenzweig (1886–1929) and Will Herberg (1909–1977) and in the dialogical thinking of Martin Buber in which God is encountered as the Eternal Thou.[20] Professor Abraham J. Heschel taught that there are three paths that lead man to the certainty of God's existence. We sense His presence in the world, in the Bible, and in sacred deeds—in other words, in worship, learning, and action. The Jewish religion discovered that the God of nature is one with the God of history, and man can know Him by doing His will.[21] This threefold path toward the realization of God's existence leads one not only to a philosophical and religious conception of God, but to one that rings authentically Jewish, one that emanates from Jewish sources and is harmonious with them.

The first way presented by Professor Heschel for discovering God is in the tradition of general philosophical speculation. It is illustrated by the Biblical verse "Lift up your eyes on high and see, Who created these?"[22] It is like the old type of proof in that it originates with the world and like the new type of proof in that it is based on human experience. It is similar to the teleological argument proving God's existence, not so much because the universe presents logical or mechanical orderliness but because of its grandeur and its sublimeness. These in turn evoke man's sense of wonder and radical amazement. This feeling of awe that man experiences is the root of faith.[23] "The ineffable in him [man] seeks a way to that which is beyond the ineffable."[24]

DIVINE ATTRIBUTES

Philosophers and theologians were not only interested in proving or disproving (or determining the impossibility of either) that God exists; they also wanted to describe the attributes of God, His qualities and characteristics. Many were adamant in their attempts to refine our conception of God and not merely accept the crude religious beliefs that were held and cherished by the masses. The rationalist thinker Achad HaAm (1856–1927), for instance, wrote that had Hillel's convert[25] appeared to him requesting to be taught the entire Torah on one leg, he would have replied, " 'You shall not make unto you a graven image, nor any manner of likeness.' [26] This is the entire Torah and the rest is commentary." In other words, to Achad HaAm, "The essence of Judaism consists in the elevation of the ideal above all material or physical forms or conceptions." [27]

Another example of Jewish philosophy's attempt to refine our concept of religion and of God relates to the notion of anthropomorphism, or the application of human form or character to God. The pre-Socratic philosopher Xenophanes satirized the Olympian gods for their immorality and anthropomorphic character, and he asserted that animals would make God in their own image if they were to paint or produce works of art—"horses like horses, cattle like cattle." [28]

Rabbi Saadia Gaon and Maimonides both were fearless fighters against anthropomorphism. The former taught that God as Creator is unlike that which he created. Rabbi Saadia preached the necessity of interpreting the language of the Scripture in a nonanthropomorphic manner that would be acceptable to the requirements of reason.[29] Maimonides devoted a good part of the beginning of his *Guide to the Perplexed* to the elucidation of Biblical terms and expressions that have an anthropomorphic connotation and to an elimination of that connotation. So adamant against anthropomorphism was Maimonides that he included God's incorporeality as one of his thirteen principles of the Jewish faith.

In connection with the topic of anthropomorphism and divine attributes, reference should be made to Professor Heschel's philosophy of Pathos, which is explained to mean that God is concerned about man and is emotionally affected by what happens in the world.[30] In contradistinction to the Stoic doctrine of apathy, Professor Heschel proposed a God of compassion; and in lieu of God as the unmoved mover, He is portrayed as the Most Moved Mover.[31] Professor Heschel tried to avoid the accusation of anthropomorphism that was leveled against him by affirming that Pathos is not an attribute, but a situation;[32] that it is not part of God's essence, but a relative state that always refers to humanity.[33] He also wrote, "To speak of God as if He were a person does not necessarily mean to personify Him, to stamp Him in the image of a person."[34] Despite these qualifications, the concept of Pathos has been considered anthropomorphic.[35] In this connection Maurice Friedman quoted Professor Heschel as saying, "Anthropomorphic language may be preferable to abstract language, for when you use abstract language you may have the illusion of adequacy."[36] Actually, Professor Heschel attempted to turn the tables on anthropomorphism by citing the biblical story that man was created in the Divine image[37] and not vice versa, and that man is commanded to be holy because God is holy[38]—an indication of theomorphic anthropology rather than of anthropomorphism.[39]

MONOTHEISM

It is generally agreed that the great contribution of the ancient Hebrews is their introducing monotheism to world civilization. The Jewish concept of monotheism includes the following three concepts: (1) There is only one God; (2) God is whole and indivisible; and (3) God is unique. The centrality of the monotheistic doctrine for Judaism is indicated by the twice-daily recital of the *Shema* prayer affirming the credence that God is one. It also is the desire of the pious Jew that at the time of death his or her last utterance should be the *Shema.*[40]

Professor Yechezkel Kaufmann took pains to show that monotheism is not a simple numerical reduction in the number of deities worshipped. He affirmed that monotheism was a revolution in man's worldview and that it is separated by an abyss from paganism. The God of the Israelites has sovereign transcendence over all, eliminating the pagan idea of a realm beyond the deity that is the source of mythology and magic. The mythological wars of the gods and the power of fate over man and gods alike are removed by the Jewish monotheistic outlook. That God is supreme and absolutely free are nonpagan ways of thinking.[41] Thus Hebrew monotheism is not merely an arithmetic reduction in the number of gods from many to One, but rather a qualitative innovation in the religious outlook and thought of mankind.

The subject of Divine attributes occupies much space in Jewish philosophical discourse. Dr. Alexander Altmann wrote that it is "based on the problem of how God, whose essence is presumed to be unknowable, can be spoken of in meaningful terms."[42] Rabbi Saadia Gaon affirmed that besides God's unity and incomparability, the attributes of vitality (life), omnipotence, and omniscience follow from His being the Creator. These three attributes, according to Rabbi Saadia, exist in the Deity simultaneously and are actually one elemental concept. Because of the limitation of human language, this one basic concept is expressed with three different words.[43]

Maimonides, always trying to present the loftiness of God and to eliminate any inklings of incorporeality from Him, formulated an influential conception of Divine attributes. Maimonides taught that God's existence is identical with His essence. His essence is absolutely simple and it excludes all positive definition. All essential divine attributes are to be understood in negative terms. When we say that God is powerful, we mean He is not weak; when we say that God is wise, we mean He is not ignorant. This doctrine of negative attributes applies to God's essence. The positive attributes found in the Bible, including the "thirteen attributes of mercy," do not describe God's essence but are to be understood as attributes or descriptions of His actions.[44]

FREEDOM OF THE WILL

The problem of human freedom of the will is a formidable one in general philosophy. Just as causality operates within nature and enables us to explain natural phenomena, so determinism found in human activity provides us with explanations of group and individual behavior. If human behavior is governed exclusively by causation and everything people do is determined (i.e., caused), is there any room within this purview for human freedom? Does man choose his destiny or is he simply another cog in the cause-and-effect process that governs natural events? It is true that man feels that he is free and makes conscious choices, but the question is whether his choices are predetermined, regardless of his realization of it or not? Immanuel Kant recognized the antinomy of freedom and necessity and concluded that freedom is an inevitable postulate of practical reason. For Kant, ethics entails obeying the categorical imperative out of a sense of duty. In order to fulfill ethical obligations, one must be free and able to do so. In other words, "ought" implies "can."[45] Akin to this type of thinking, Rabbi Saadia Gaon wrote that since God gave men commandments and holds them responsible for their obedience, it would be an act of Divine injustice if men lacked the freedom to choose between alternatives. Rabbi Saadia also recognized human awareness of that freedom as evidence for it.[46] In addition, he quoted the biblical passage "See, I set before you this day life and good, and death and evil. . . . Therefore choose life."[47]

There is a deterministic view expressed in the Talmud by Rabbi Chanina bar Chama (early third century), who said, "No man brushes his finger here on earth, unless it was so decreed against him in heaven."[48] However, in another quotation from Rabbi Chanina, he expressed the delicate balance between determinism and freedom: "Everything is in the hands of Heaven except the fear of Heaven."[49]

If free will presents a difficult problem for general philosophy, it spells double trouble for Jewish thought, which also has to reconcile the apparently incompatible doctrines of human freedom and Divine foreknowledge and omniscience. This problem is usually represented by the pithy statement of Rabbi Akiva, "Everything is foreseen [by God], yet free will is granted [to man]."[50] Rabbi Saadia Gaon believed that God's foreknowledge has no causal bearing on the alternatives man chooses. Maimonides opined that since God's knowledge is essentially different from human knowledge, it is possible to hold on to both horns of the dilemma. Gersonides and Rabbi Chasdai Crescas took opposite sides on this issue. The former limited God's knowledge of the sublunar world to generalities, thus allowing for human freedom of the will. Crescas, on the other hand, accepted thorough Divine omniscience and advocated that human acts are determined.[51]

MIRACLES

From the problem of free will and determinism, we turn to the question of miracles in a universe governed by regularity and natural law. From a naturalistic perspective, it is absurd to accept the occurrence of miracles or breaks in nature. If nature is supreme, how can there be a suspension or alteration of natural laws? From a theistic point of view, although there are problems aplenty the logical impossibility of the occurrence of miracles disappears. In a metanatural or supernatural world where God is the Creator of nature, there is a rational possibility for miracles to take place. It should be noted that the Rabbis regarded all existence as miraculous, not only those events that are breaches of nature. In the daily *Modim* prayer we recite, "In every generation we will thank You and recount Your praise ... for Your miracles which are daily with us, and for Your continual wonders and favors—evening, morning, and noon." However, the Rabbis recognized the difference between miracles within nature and those that are contrary to the laws of nature. There is a rabbinic view that supernatural miracles, those that are breaks of nature, were predetermined at the time of creation and are not actual changes in Divine will or ad hoc violations of the natural order.[52] "At the creation God made a condition with the sea that it should be divided for the passage of the children of Israel; with the sun and moon to stand still at the bidding of Joshua; with the ravens to feed Elijah; with fire not to injure Chananiah, Mishael, and Azariah; with the lions not to harm Daniel; and with the fish to spew out Jonah."[53]

Interesting is the biblical view that miracles can be performed for idolatrous purposes. Here is the biblical passage: "If there appear among you a prophet or a dream diviner and he gives you a sign or a portent, saying, 'Let us follow and worship another god'—whom you have not experienced—even if the sign or portent that he named to you comes true, do not heed the words of that prophet or that dream diviner. For the Lord your God is testing you to see whether you really love the Lord your God with all your heart and soul." [54] Similarly, Rabbi Saadia Gaon wrote that one must hold on to rational convictions, such as that truth is good and lying is reprehensible, even if miracles were performed to support contrary irrational doctrines. [55]

RELIGION AND SCIENCE

Concluding this chapter will be the philosophical problem of the relationship between religion and science. The growth, development, and spectacular success of modern science and technology have presented religion with serious challenges to its intellectual respectability. This problem is not entirely new, for science and philosophy have always put some pressure upon religion. For instance, Maimonides and Gersonides wrestled with the then-prevailing Aristotelian view concerning the eternity of matter, which conflicted with the description of the creation of the world *ex nihilo* as expounded in the book of Genesis. Actually a religion like Judaism that accepts the Divine inspiration of the Bible "is likely to run into trouble when scriptural pronouncements contradict the findings of science." [56] The following are ways that Jewish and other religious thinkers have dealt with the challenges presented by science: (1) The twofold doctrine, or the "double truth" theory, that was held in Jewish philosophy by Rabbi Isaac Albalag (thirteenth century), implies that the truths of religion and those of science or philosophy can coexist side by side, even if they contradict each other. A version of this doctrine is that religion and science have different goals and their teachings have little or nothing to do with each other. (2) The theories of science differ from each other and vary from one time to another. Accordingly, scientific teachings accepted presently may be subject to change in the future, whereas those of religion are permanent. (3) Allegorization of those aspects of religious teachings that are counterindicated by science. Maimonides considered the biblical teaching of creation more probable than the Aristotelian theory of the eternity of the universe. He boldly stated that had the latter view been proven philosophically, he would have interpreted the Bible in a manner agreeable with it, just as he interpreted the anthropomorphic terminology of the Bible allegorically.[57]

This method of allegorizing or adjusting religious teachings whenever they encounter difficulties from science or from everyday experience was criticized by analytical philosophers such as Anthony Flew. The complaint they uttered is that religious thinking allows for no possible falsifiability, so, Flew wanted to know, "What would have to occur or to have occurred to constitute *disproof*" of any religious teaching or doctrine? When a religious teaching, such as God's love for man, is construed in a manner unlike human love or as inscrutable love, there is qualification after qualification until the religious teaching "dies the death of a thousand qualifications."[58] Actually, a similar question can be raised about what would have to occur to constitute *proof* of religious teaching or doctrine? Professor Heschel once remarked that if God were to appear on television, people would deny Him because our age is so permeated with agnosticism and atheism that people would do anything in order not to believe. In reply to Flew, it could also be stated that science as well as religion qualifies itself when new evidence is presented, and older theories have been modified or even abandoned. This does not invalidate the respectability of science. It might also be argued that this method of qualification, adjustment, and allegorization is actually a strength of Judaism and not a weakness. It is a philosophical, though not Halachic, outlet that allows for the intellectual integrity of the Jewish religion as it faced and faces all sorts of challenges from science, from historical study, and from an unforeseeable future to come. It is to the credit of such thinkers like Rabbi Saadia Gaon and Maimonides who clearly formulated and verbalized an invigorating and rational methodology that enables ancient Judaism to be eternally current and to be as young as it thinks.

ENDNOTES

1. William P. Alston, "Philosophy of Religion, Problems of," in *Encyclopedia of Philosophy*, vol. 6, p. 285, and John Hick, *Philosophy of Religion* (Englewood Cliffs: Prentice-Hall, 1963), p. 1.

2. Anselm of Canterbury, *Proslogium*, beginning.

3. R. E. Allen, "Anselm, St.," in *Encyclopedia of Philosophy*, vol. 1, p. 162.

4. Ex. 24:7

5. Emil L. Fackenheim, *Encounters Between Judaism and Modern Philosophy* (New York: Basic Books, 1973), p. 3.

6. Alston, op. cit., pp. 285–286.

7. William P. Alston, "Religion," in *Encyclopedia of Philosophy*, vol. 7, pp. 140–145.

8. At the beginning of the Jewish Law chapter.

9. San. 37a.

10. Rabbi Joseph B. Soloveitchik, "The First Jewish Grandfather," in Abraham R. Besdin, ed., *Man of Faith in the Modern World: Reflections of the Rav* (Hoboken, NJ: Ktav, 1989), pp. 21–23. See also Abraham Joshua Heschel, "Toward an Understanding of Halacha," in Susannah Heschel, ed., *Moral Grandeur and Spiritual Audacity* (New York: Farrar, Straus, & Giroux, 1996), p. 142.

11. Maimonides, commentary to ch. 10 of Mishna Sanhedrin. The summary of Maimonides' "Thirteen Principles of Faith" quoted here is from Philip Birnbaum, *A Book of Jewish Concepts* (New York: Hebrew Publishing Co, 1964), p. 50.

12. For a brief consideration of principles of Jewish faith, see Alexander Altmann, "Articles of Faith," in *Encyclopedia Judaica*, vol. 3, pp. 654–660.

13. Chab. 2:4 and Mak. 24a.

14. Rashi's commentary to Ex. 24:12. See also Judah David Eisenstein, "Aseret HaDibrot," (New York: Hebrew Publishing Co., 1907-1913), in *Otzar Yisrael Encyclopedia* (Hebrew), vol. 8, pp. 154–168.

15. Alston, "Philosophy of Religion, Problems of," op. cit., p. 286.

16. Marvin Fox, "God," in *Encyclopedia Judaica*, vol. 7 pp. 657–661.

17. Hick, op, cit., p. 47.

18. Upon Pascal's death, this confession of faith was found on a piece of parchment sewn in the lining of his coat. See Hick, ibid., p. 61.

19. Julius Guttmann, *Philosophies of Judaism* English translation by David W. Silverman, (New York: Holt, Rinehart and Winston, 1964), pp. 122–125, and Isaac Husik, *A History of Medieval Jewish Philosophy* (Philadelphia: Jewish Publication Society, 1948), pp. 157–159.

20. Fox, op. cit., p. 664. See Franz Rosenzweig, *The Star of Redemption* (Boston: Beacon Press, 1972); Will Herberg, *Judaism and Modern Man* (Philadelphia: Jewish Publication Society and New York: Meridian, 1960); Martin Buber, *I and Thou* (New York: Charles Scribner's Sons, 1958).

21. Abraham, J. Heschel, *God in Search of Man* (Philadelphia: Jewish Publication Society, 1955), pp. 30–32.

22. Is. 40:26.

23. Heschel, op. cit., p. 77.

24. Ibid., p. 353.

25. Shab. 31a.

26. Ex. 20:4.

27. Achad HaAm, *Al Parashat Derachim*, 4, is cited in Louis Jacobs, "Judaism," in *Encyclopedia Judaica*, vol. 10, p. 384.

28. Milton C. Nahm, ed., *Selections from Early Greek Philosophy*, 3rd ed. (New York: Appleton-Century-Crofts, 1947), p. 109, fragments 5, 6, and 7.

29. Saadia Gaon, *The Book of Beliefs and Opinions* (New Haven: Yale, 1948), pp. 111–112, Treatise II, ch. 8.

30. Abraham J. Heschel, *The Prophets* (Philadelphia: Jewish Publication Society, 1962), pp. 224, 483.

31. Ibid., pp. 252–259. See also Fritz A. Rothschild, ed., *Between God and Man* (New York: Free Press, 1959), introduction.

32. Heschel, *The Prophets*, op. cit. p. 225.

33. Ibid., p. 231.

34. Ibid., p. 273.

35. Eliezer Berkovits, *Major Themes in Modern Philosophies of Judaism* (Hoboken, NJ: Ktav, 1974), pp. 198, 205.

36. Maurice Friedman, *Abraham Joshua Heschel and Elie Wiesel* (New York: Farrar, Straus, Giroux, 1987), p. 69.

37. Gen. 1:27.

38. Lev. 19:2.

39. Heschel, *The Prophets*, op. cit., p. 260.

40. See Ber. 61b, which describes Rabbi Akiva reciting the *Shema* as he was being tortured to death by the Romans. He expired with the word "one" on his lips and said that he was finally fulfilling the commandment of loving God with his entire soul (Deut. 6:5).

41. Yechezkel Kaufmann, "The Biblical Age," in Leo W. Schwarz, ed., *Great Ages and Ideas of the Jewish People* (New York: Random House, 1956), pp. 12–13.

42. Alexander Altmann, "Attributes of God," in *Encyclopedia Judaica*, vol. 7, p. 664.

43. Saadia Gaon, op. cit., pp. 101–102, Treatise II, ch. 4.

44. Maimonides, *Guide for the Perplexed*, Part 1, chs. 51–60; Alexander Altmann, "Attributes of God," op. cit., pp. 666–667; Guttmann, op. cit., pp. 158–163.

45. Raziel Abelson, "Ethics, History of," in *Encyclopedia of Philosophy*, vol. 3, p. 96, and Edwin A. Burtt, *Types of Religious Philosophy* (New York: Harper & Brothers, 1939), pp. 269–270. One is reminded of the bon mot "Man must be free; there is no choice."

46. Saadia Gaon, op. cit., Treatise IV, chs. 3 and 4.

47. Deut. 30:15–19.

48. Chul. 7b.

49. Ber. 33b.

50. Avot 3:19. For a different interpretation of this Mishna see Ephraim E. Urbach, *The Sages* (Cambridge: Harvard University Press, 1987), p. 257 (Translator is Israel Abrahams, trans. from Hebrew). Prof. Urbach maintained that the verb *tzafoh* (to see or foresee) was used in mishnaic times to mean seeing in the present and not foreseeing what will be in the future. He wrote, "The context

of the Mishna likewise shows that Rabbi Akiva's intention was not to resolve the contradiction between [God's] foreknowledge and [man's] free will, but to make man realize his responsibility for his actions." In other words, everything is seen and man is able to choose.

51. Shlomo Pines, "Free Will," in *Encyclopedia Judaica*, vol. 7, pp. 125–129.

52. Maimonides, *Guide*, op. cit., Part II, ch. 29, and his commentary to Avot 5:6. See also article on "Miracles" in *Encyclopedia Judaica*, vol. 12, pp. 73–79. Perhaps the two Hebrew words for miracle, *peleh* (wonder) and *nes* (something outstanding) reflect this distinction between miracles within nature and those that break natural law?

53. Gen. R. 5:4, quoted in A. Cohen, *Everyman's Talmud* (New York: Dutton, 1949), p. 11.

54. Deut. 13:2–4.

55. Saadia Gaon, op. cit., Treatise III, ch. 8, p. 164.

56. J. J. C. Smart, "Religion and Science," in *The Encyclopedia of Philosophy*, vol. 7, p. 159.

57. Maimonides, *Guide*, op. cit., Part 2, ch. 25.

58. Anthony Flew, "Theology and Falsification," in Anthony Flew, and Alasdair Macintyre, eds., *New Essays in Philosophical Theology* (New York: Macmillan, 1955), pp. 96–99.

SEVEN

JEWISH AESTHETICS

One does not usually associate aesthetics and the arts with the Jewish religion and Jewish life. A number of reasons account for this phenomenon. The first is the seemingly iconoclastic nature of the second of the Ten Commandments, which prohibits the making of sculptured images or any likeness of anything in heaven or earth.[1] Another reason for the alleged Jewish disassociation from aesthetic activity is the primacy accorded by Judaism to Torah learning, categorizing other pursuits as *bittul Torah*, or time taken away from more important Torah study.[2] The poverty always rampant in Jewish ghettos and *shtetlach* also served as a deterrent to aesthetic creativity. Additionally, life in exile, with wanderings of Jewish populations from one place to another, impeded upon the growth and development of artistic endeavors. When one is indigent and under constant threat of persecution or forced migration, he usually does not give prime time and consideration to the arts and probably does not pack aesthetic objects to take along while looking for a new place to call home.

JEWISH LIFE AND THE ARTS

Despite all this, it would be erroneous to divorce aesthetics and art from Jewish life. Thanks to surprising archaeological findings, we know of ancient synagogue murals and mosaics and of sarcophagi that depict not only religious symbols but also human and animal forms. Other examples of Jewish visual art include the Temple in Jerusalem, which was certainly built to be aesthetically pleasing;[3] biblical royal residences; ancient and modern synagogue buildings; paintings found in illuminated Jewish manuscripts and books; and beautiful religious ceremonial objects. The modern era has witnessed the cultivation and proliferation of traditional Jewish art, and many Jewish painters, sculptors, and architects have contributed major works in all artistic categories, religious and secular.[4] Jews have also made musical contributions, such as the liturgical singing of the Levites in the Temple, the cantillation of the weekly reading of the Torah and Prophets, cantorial music, hasidic melodies, folk songs, etc. In the field of literature, it is sufficient to mention the Bible, which contains both poetry and narrative of the highest aesthetic caliber.

That aesthetics plays an important role within Judaism is illustrated by the concept of *hiddur mitzvah*, which implies the obligation to perform commandments in an aesthetically pleasing manner. This concept is derived from the biblical verse "This is my God and I will glorify Him."[5] We are told to construct a beautiful *sukkah*, utilize a beautiful *etrog*, a beautiful shofar, a beautiful *sefer Torah*, etc. We are exhorted to spend up to one-third more money in order to procure more beautiful religious artifacts required for the performance of commandments.[6]

A problem in aesthetics, as elsewhere, is definition: What is meant by aesthetics and what is art? The related question can be asked: What is Jewish art? Must Jewish art have a Jewish theme and be created by an artist who is Jewish, or is only one of the requirements sufficient to categorize art as being Jewish?[7]

A central philosophical problem of aesthetics is whether beauty or aesthetic properties are inherent in an object or reside in the mind of the beholder, whether beauty is an objective quality or a subjective one. People argue and disagree about the aesthetic value of art objects, and the tastes of one generation differ from those of another. However, there is some general consensus among connoisseurs that some objets d'art are masterpieces and belong in museums while others fall short in smaller or larger degrees.

We see a reflection of this philosophical controversy in connection with the holiday of Sukkot. With regard to the *etrog* and *sukkah*, allowance is made for beautifying the commandments on both objective and subjective levels. Suppose a person thinks that a chubby, smooth *etrog* with a little dot toward the top is cute or aesthetically appealing. That is not acceptable, according to the Halacha. There are definite objective criteria delineating what constitutes a beautiful *etrog*, such as it should not have spots, particularly toward the top; it should not be smooth; and it should be narrow, in the shape of a tower (*migdal*).[8] Aesthetically, it is not sufficient that it qualify as kosher. On the other hand, we are also enjoined to beautify the sukkah, and may decorate it according to our own personal, individual aesthetic preferences—with embroidered curtains, posters, pictures, or old *lulavim* on the walls; or with fruits and other objects hanging from the *schach*, or roof. The last is perhaps an early example of kinetic art, in the spirit of Alexander Calder. The point is that when it comes to beautifying the *sukkah*, subjective taste is acceptable, unlike the objective criteria that determine the qualities of a beautiful *etrog*.

Two comments regarding modern art might be of interest in the area of Jewish aesthetics. In deference to the second commandment, there is a custom of slitting off the nose of a sculpture in order to make it nonrepresentational. Professor Steven Schwarzchild (1924–1989) identified this as one of the earliest examples of the "modernist" revolution in art and wrote, "What is usually called 'distortion' is thus quintessential and aboriginal Jewish aesthetics."[9] It should be noted that this distortion via nose slitting is antithetical to distortion as utilized by Expressionist artists. The latter use distortion to *emphasize* the artist's feelings or his message, whereas Jewish nose slitting distortion aims to *eliminate* the feeling or message inherent in or evoked by the art object. Thus, nose slitting as distortion is anti-Expressionistic.

The other comment regarding Jewish tradition and modern art concerns the nonobjective or nonrepresentational aspect of modernism. Its being imageless is amusingly consistent with the iconoclastic requirements of the second commandment, even according to its most stringent interpretation.[10]

It is sometimes maintained that Jewish religious art is really craft and not art per se[11] because religious ceremonial objects—even beautiful ones such as *menorot,* kiddush cups, spice boxes, etc.—are created by trained (often talented) craftsmen, rather than by artists. Although there is much truth to this contention, there are many examples of Jewish religious art objects that emanate from artistic inspiration and not from mere trained workmanship. Jewish manuscript illumination is by and large an example of Jewish art, not Jewish craft. The master artist and craftsman mentioned in the Bible in connection with the construction of the ark and the tent of meeting is Bezalel, the son of Uri. Even though the Bible attributes to him consummate craftsmanship ("skill, ability, and knowledge in every kind of craft"), he was also an artist "called by name" and filled with the "spirit of God."[12]

Another disclaimer applied to Jewish art is that it is not art for its own sake, but is the handmaiden of the Jewish religion.[13] Up until the modern period, there is more than a modicum of truth to this assertion. But so what! Much of art brings home a message or has an ulterior purpose. The same criticism, if that is what it is, can be made of Christian art and other religious art, but this does not detract from the aesthetic value of the artistic works themselves.

There are a number of ways in which the freedom of an artist is constrained. The composer of opera cannot allow his imagination to have free reign; his or her music is limited by or must comply with the chosen libretto. The aesthetics of architecture is frequently judged by the saying "Form follows function." When an architect draws up a plan, he or she must have practical as well as aesthetic goals in mind; for instance, one is not free to design a synagogue that looks like a factory building.

Much of Jewish art suffers from similar limitations. When the prophets delivered their prophecies to the people, their language was limited by their message. Nevertheless, they produced a most beautiful and sublime literature. That the Bible is a religious creation, and is not for art's sake, does not detract from its great artistic value. Aspects of Jewish music also have ulterior purposes besides the aesthetic one.[14] An example is hasidic music: The enchanting, brief hasidic melodies and tunes are repeated over and over again in order to evoke a religious experience and serve as aids to attaining ecstasy. The Jewish tune also serves as an enjoyable mnemonic device for students who study the Talmud with its own unique chant, and the cantillation of the weekly Torah reading in the synagogue helps the reader and listener remember the words recited besides adding beauty to the Torah reading itself. The music and the melody in these instances are bound to textual material, but they nonetheless inculcate an aesthetic dimension within the study hall and place of worship. Clearly an artist is not always neutral or free to create whatever he wishes out of a vacuum. What constitutes a work of art, including Jewish art, is that it should have aesthetic value, that it should disseminate visual, aural, or literary delight to those who come in contact with it.

MEANING IN JEWISH ART AND LITERATURE

A topic in general aesthetics deals with meaning in art. It is questionable whether painting, sculpture, or music convey meaning. Line, color, and musical notes do not contain a message that one person can verbalize to another. One branch of aesthetics, though, by its very nature does consist of meaning, and that of course is literature.[15] Since Judaism is text centered, with study and the literary medium being quintessential components of Jewish life, it is appropriate to deal with meaning and Jewish literature.

It is an exaggeration of the truth to assert that Jewish literature is the Bible, "while the rest is commentary thereof; go and learn it."[16] Professor Simon Rawidowicz (1896–1957) wrote, "When one thinks of Israel's spiritual and literary work through the ages—its essence, manifestations, and style—one is faced at first thought with a peculiar double-layered phenomenon: a 'text' on the one hand, its 'commentary' on the other. . . . Technically the 'text' is the Bible, all the rest is 'commentary.' "[17] With the passage of time, some of the commentaries themselves became text for further commentary.

What kind of meaning can one attain or aspire to attain from a document, particularly one that is many centuries old? Basically the meaning and significance of a text or any work of art is determined by any or all of the following three factors: the intent of the creator; the content of the work itself; and the relevance to the reader, viewer, or listener.[18]

The problem of intentionality in aesthetics, which can apply to legal interpretation as well,[19] is a complex one. One issue is whether the product of an artistic or literary creation is what the artist or author originally intended it to be when he or she started out. Can the viewer or reader ever know if the final result equals the initial intent? Probably not, if not so informed explicitly by the artist or author. Also, is it possible for a reader who interprets a literary work to comprehend fully or experience exactly what the author had in mind or what the author felt? The "Intentional Fallacy"[20] asserts that in these matters there is an unbridgeable gap between the artist or author and his or her audience. On the other hand, no author would write if he thought his readers could not know what he meant to convey. If he is misunderstood, the author might be faulted for not expressing himself more clearly, but it is not because of a logical impossibility of being understood. Authors write with the assumption and belief that it is possible to have an identity equation or great similarity between the mind of the writer and the mind of the reader, or between their emotional experiences.[21] The problems involved in literary understanding compound and magnify when dealing with works written in ancient times, at other places, and in different languages.

A technique utilized to both understand and appreciate a work of art, music, or literature is investigation of its background material. This includes biographical and psychological knowledge about the author or artist and philological, historical, and sociological knowledge related to the work itself. These types of study are interesting and important as ends in themselves and as helpmates toward one's understanding of aesthetic objects. However, in the areas of aesthetics, criticism, and to a large extent meaning, this type of investigation can be carried to excess, and the work of art slips away tangentially from being the center of attraction to becoming a pretext for all kinds of scholarly monographs and publications. Wellek and Austin wrote, "Literary history has been so preoccupied with the setting of a work of literature that its attempts at an analysis of the works themselves have been slight in comparison with the enormous efforts expended on the study of environment."[22] They advocated relegating to the background such "studies in the psychology of the reader and the spectator or the author and the artist as well as studies in the cultural and social background, however illuminating they may be from their own point of view."[23] They pointedly asserted, "One must never forget that the establishment of a different date of authorship does not dispose of the actual question of criticism. Chatterton's poems are neither worse nor better for having been written in the eighteenth century."[24] The implications and ramifications of discussions on intent, content, and relevance are pertinent to biblical exegesis and to how we approach any work of art or written text, Jewish or general.

It has been observed that "One might very roughly periodize the history of modern literary theory in three stages: a preoccupation with the author (Romanticism and the nineteenth century); an exclusive concern with the text (New Criticism); and a marked shift of attention to the reader over recent years."[25] A distinction has been made between meaning and significance is textual interpretation. A text might have one meaning intended by the author and many interpretations or significances determined by its various readers at different times. However, legitimate interpretations must move within the "system of typical expectations and probabilities" that the author's meaning permits.[26] Much more power is given to the reader by the deconstruction theory of Jacques Derrida (b. 1930). According to him, the text does not embody or convey meaning; "It [the text] is the scene of activity in which the reader inscribes meaning,"[27] the reader thus becoming the writer.[28] This type of thinking that empowers the reader, giving to him literary creativity, has bestowed added popularity in some circles upon the old midrashic method of textual interpretation.

The Midrash frequently gives multiple, variegated, and sometimes contradictory interpretations of biblical verses. This runs counter to customary, logical, and strict thinking, but if we legitimate significances alongside with meaning and transform the reader into an author, midrash as literature and methodology again becomes a contemporary literary genre. An essential distinction, nevertheless, must be made between rabbinic midrash and so-called contemporary midrash. The former adheres very carefully to E. D. Hirsch's remark cited above in that it operates within the "system of typical expectations and probabilities" that Biblical meaning permits. Harold Fish has pointed out that the midrash of the rabbis, although "open" like its contemporary version, is also governed by the unlimited authority inherent in the prime biblical text.[29]

The methodological variations within Jewish interpretation of Scripture are frequently described by the acronym PaRDeS.[30] The text can be interpreted in a fourfold manner: literally, homiletically, esoterically, and with veiled allusions; the last for example, referring to *gematriot*, or numerical equivalents of biblical words or phrases. Professor Rawidowicz distinguished between two types of commentary: The first is *explicatio* and *commentatio* and the second *interpretatio*.[31] Commentary via *explicatio* seeks to uncover and explain, paying attention to form, content, and historical background. In contradistinction, *interpretatio* exegesis centers around the soul of the text, its main purpose, and essence. *Interpretatio* aspires to make the implicit in the text explicit, to spell out that which is implied.[32] Rawidowicz maintained that inherent in most kinds of *explicatio* there is some, and usually much, *interpretatio*. He compared *explicatio* to *melacha* (work) and *interpretatio* to *chochma* (wisdom),[33] obviously implying the superiority of the latter.

A different view concerning the relative value of *pshat* (literal commentary) and *drash* (homiletical interpretation) is expressed by Professor E. Z. Melamed (1903–1994). He believed that *pshat* attempts to arrive at the intentions and meaning of the creator of the text, whereas *drash* allows personal interpretations, whether conscious or not, to play a part in exegesis. *Pshat*, according to Melamed, is objective, and *drash* is subjective. He held that the job of the *pshat* exegete is more difficult than that of the *drash* commentator. This is so because the one who interprets according to *pshat* has to cross over different geographical locations and go back to different time periods than the one in which he or she lives in order to understand the text in its primary or pristine meaning.[34]

It is true that the *drash* exegete is usually familiar with the simple or literal meaning of the text. However, he or she tries to extrapolate any and all meanings that can be squeezed out of the text in order to show how the ancient document is relevant and has something significant to offer contemporary needs and tastes. In this manner the text grows in interpretation with the passage of time. Of course, there is *drash* in which the exegete reads his or her own thoughts into the text to a greater degree than he or she reads thoughts out of the text. When this infidelity to the text occurs, the *drash* is of an inferior quality.

It is noteworthy that *pshat* and *drash* are not only methods of interpretation; they sometimes also contain within themselves an aesthetic quality. This manifests itself when we say, "That is a beautiful *pshat*," or "That is a beautiful piece of *drush* (*drash*)." However, the originator of the beautiful *pshat* is more like a scientist who *discovers* something beautiful, whereas the author of the beautiful *drush* is more like an artist who *creates* the aesthetic interpretation of the text.

In vogue since the late 1960s is the literary method of biblical interpretation. Since the Bible is in the mode of literature, it is being interpreted by means of literary canons or techniques. Viewing the Bible as literary art does not detract from its religious dimensions, but rather enhances it.[35] Professor Robert Alter (b. 1936) does not view the Bible's literary character as merely one of its several characteristics. He prefers "to insist on a complete interfusion of literary art with theological, moral, or historical vision, the fullest perception of the latter dependent on the fullest grasp of the former."[36]

BEAUTY AND UGLINESS

A subject sometimes discussed in aesthetics is the antithetical counterpart of beauty, namely ugliness.[37] Actually, ugliness is not necessarily the antonym of beauty. If beauty is conceived as that which has aesthetic value, an object lacking aesthetic value is not necessarily ugly but rather aesthetically neutral. It should be mentioned that ugliness oddly enough sometimes evokes aesthetic pleasure. Two examples of pleasing ugliness would be tragic drama and Picasso's *Demoiselles d'Avignon*, the latter recognized as "the watershed between the old pictorial world and the new."[38] Also, the term ugly frequently carries an ethical connotation, not just an aesthetic one, such as referring to murder as an ugly deed.

What does this discussion about aesthetic ugliness have to do with Jewish aesthetics? Two concepts come to mind. There are several prohibitions cited in the Pentateuch described by the words *sheketz* and *toeiva*, each meaning abomination. The terms are utilized only in connection with the following: idolatry,[39] sacrificing defiled animals on the altar,[40] dietary laws,[41] sexual aberrations such as incest and homosexuality,[42] and utilizing false weights and measures.[43] It would seem that engaging in these abominable acts is not only a religious and moral vice but also an ugly and reprehensible activity, one that is aesthetically repulsive. Interestingly, forced converts and Marranos, when they abandoned Jewish practices, had the most difficulty regarding nonkosher food consumption, particularly eating pork, which they found especially repulsive[44]—seemingly aesthetically so.

It sometimes happens that ugliness or aesthetic revulsion permeates a person's psyche when he or she sins or at the conclusion of a life of iniquity. Rabbi Joseph B. Soloveitchik, the expositor par excellence of the concept of repentance or *Teshuva*, portrayed two facets of the mentality of penitents.[45] Sometimes an individual examines his or her sinful actions and intellectually realizes that he or she did wrong and seeks to repent.[46] Then there is the person who after sinning is so repelled by it emotionally that he or she feels disgust, great shame, and abhorrence for the ugliness of the the deed committed, as illustrated by the hatred by

Amnon for Tamar that was greater than the love he had for her before the episode that caused the hatred.[47] This second type of penitent has a "negative aesthetic reaction" to the transgression, an "anti-aesthetic experience" of the sin.[48]

TORAH STUDY AND AESTHETIC DELIGHT

If one were to inquire what activity Judaism cherishes most, a strong case can be made for study of Torah. Indeed, the *Mishna* does inform us that of the many virtues, such as honoring parents, doing acts of kindness, hospitality to strangers, visiting the sick, and devotion in prayer, Torah study is the most important, or at least equal to the rest.[49] While we think of study as an intellectual activity, it also has an aesthetic aspect. Professor John Hospers wrote that the range of aesthetics is not limited to the actual perceptual. "When we enjoy or appreciate the elegance of a mathematical proof, it would surely seem that our enjoyment is aesthetic, although the object of that enjoyment is not perceptual at all: it is the complex relation among abstract ideas or propositions, not the marks on paper or the blackboard, that we are apprehending aesthetically."[50] Undoubtedly many who study Torah acquire aesthetic delight from it. They refer to the sweetness of the Torah, that her paths are pleasant,[51] and pray daily that God should make the words of the Torah pleasant in our mouths.[52] Rabbi Chaim ben Atar (1696–1742) in his *Ohr HaChaim* commented, "Were people to realize the sweetness and pleasure of Torah, they would pursue it with the most intense fervor and determination."[53] He also declared, "One who toils over Torah study will taste a sweetness like a honey delicacy."[54] The Chazon Ish (1878–1953) wrote in a letter, "Sweet experiences can impart a sense of pleasure to a person's body and to all his limbs in a limited way; but this pleasure can never compete with the noble pleasures of toiling for wisdom, in which the soul of man is uplifted above, where it absorbs pleasure from the glow of elevated wisdom."[55]

Although there is room for aesthetics or beauty within Judaism, it nevertheless occupies an ancillary role and is not of its core. Dr. Samuel

Rosenblatt described this phenomenon when he said of the holiday of Chanukah that it commemorates the victory of the Jewish way of life that subscribes to the beauty of holiness over the Greek or Hellenistic civilization that extols the holiness of beauty.[56]

ENDNOTES

1. Ex. 20:4–5; Deut. 5:8–9.

2. The same point was made in the Jewish History chapter.

3. The Talmud states, "It used to be said: He who has not seen the Temple of Herod has never seen a beautiful building. Of what did he build it? Rabbah said: Of yellow and white marble. Some say of blue, yellow, and white marble.... He originally intended to cover it with gold, but the rabbis advised him not to, since it was beautiful the way it was, looking like the waves of the sea." B. B. 4a and Suk. 51b.

4. See "Art," in *Encyclopedia Judaica*, vol. 3; pp. 499–614 Robert Gordis and Moshe Davidowitz, eds., *Art in Judaism* (New York, National Council on Art in Jewish Life and Judaism, 1975); Cecil Roth, *Jewish Art* (Tel Aviv: Massadah, 1961); Grace Cohen Grossman, *Jewish Art*, No place of publication (Hugh Lauter Levin Associates, 1995).

5. Ex. 15:2.

6. B. K. 9b. For a discussion of *hiddur mitzvah* and its various ramifications, see "Hiddur Mitzvah," in *Encyclopedia Talmudit*, vol. 8 (Hebrew), (Jerusalem: Hotzaat Entziklopedia Talmudit), pp. 271–283.

7. Steven S. Schwarzschild, "Aesthetics," in Arthur A Cohen and Paul Mendes-Flohr, eds., *Contemporary Jewish Religious Thought* (New York: Free Press, 1987), p. 1.

8. Eliyahu Kitov, *Sefer HaTodaah*, part 1, (Jerusalem: Machon LiHotzaat Sefarim,

1964), p. 90 (An English translation is available). See also "Etrog," in *Encyclopedia Talmudit,* vol. 2, pp. 309–315.

9. Schwarzschild, op. cit., p. 2.

10. Ibid., p. 6. See also Avram Kampf, *Jewish Experience in The Art of the Twentieth Century* (Hadley, Mass.: Bergin & Garvey, 1984), p. 201.

11. Schwarzschild, op. cit., p. 2.

12. Ex. 31:1–5 and Ex. 35:30–35.

13. Schwarzschild, op. cit., p. 2.

14. Moseh Idel, "Music," in Cohen and Mendes-Flohr, op. cit., pp. 635–642. See also Hanoch Avenary, "Music," in *Encyclopedia Judaica,* vol. 12, pp. 580, 613–614, 637–639.

15. John Hospers, "Aesthetics, Problems in," in *The Encyclopedia of Philosophy,* vol. 1, p. 42.

16. Shab. 31a.

17. Simon Rawidowicz, "On Interpretation," in Nahum N. Glatzer, ed., *Studies in Jewish Thought* (Philadelphia: Jewish Publication Society, 1974), p. 45.

18. Rabbi Aharon Lichtenstein dealt with this topic in a 1984 lecture entitled "Torat Chesed, Torat Emet," where he equated *Torat emet* with the original divine intent and *Torat chesed* with the license of interpretation, illustrated by the dictum of the rabbis in Eruv. 13b concerning the differences of opinion between the disciples of Hillel and Shamai that "both are the words of the living God." He explained that different interpretations are latent in the text in potentia. However, he issued a caveat for more stringent and exact exegetical methods when it comes to halachic or legal matters. A cassette tape (not particularly clear audibly) of Rabbi Lichtenstein's address is available from the Rabbinic Alumni Office of Yeshiva University, Tape no. 283.

19. See the chapter on Jewish Law.

20. W. K. Wimsatt, and Monroe Beardsley, "The Intentional Fallacy," *Sewanee Review* (1946) pp. 468–488, reprinted frequently.

21. John Wisdom, *Other Minds* (Oxford: Basil Blackwell, 1956).

22. Rene Wellek, and Warren Austin, *Theory of Literature* (New York: Harcourt, Brace & World, Harvest Books, 1956), p. 127.

23. Ibid., p. 119.

24. Ibid., p. 57.

25. Terry Eagleton, *Literary Theory: An Introduction,* 2nd ed. (Minneapolis, MN: University of Minnesota, 1996), p. 64.

26. Ibid., p. 58, describing the views of E. D. Hirsch, Jr. in *Validity in Interpretation* (New Haven: Yale University Press, 1967). Of interest in this regard is the famous passage from San. 34a: " 'Is not my word like a hammer that breaketh the rock in pieces?' (Jer. 23:29)—as the hammer causes numerous sparks to flash off, so is a Scriptural verse capable of many interpretations."

27. Edward L. Greenstein, "Deconstruction and Biblical Narrative," in Steven Kepnes, ed., *Interpreting Judaism in a Postmodern Age* (New York: New York University Press, 1996), p. 31.

28. Ibid. and John Lechte, *Fifty Key Contemporary Thinkers* (London and New York: Routledge, 1995), p. 109.

29. Harold Fish, "The Hermeneutic Text in Robinson Crusoe," in Geoffrey H. Hartman and Sanford Budick, eds., *Midrash and Literature* (New Haven: Yale University Press, 1986), pp. 231–232.

30. PaRDeS refers to *pshat*, the literal meaning; *remez*, the veiled allusions like numerical equivalents of words; *drash*, homiletical interpretation; and *sod*, esoteric interpretation. Rabbi Bachya ben Asher (thirteenth century) in the introduction to his Torah commentary recognized four modes of interpretation: (1) *pshat*, (2) *midrash*, (3) *sechel* (rational or philosophical interpretation), and (4) *sod* (mystical interpretation).

31. Rawidowicz, op. cit., p. 47.

32. Ibid., pp. 47–48.

33. Ibid., pp. 49–50.

34. Ezra-Zion Melamed, *Meforshei HaMikra*, vol. 1 (Jerusalem: Magnes Press, 1978), pp. 5–6.

35. Robert Alter, *The Art of Biblical Narrative* (New York: Basic Books, 1981), p. 12.

36. Ibid., p. 19.

37. Jerome Stolnitz, "Ugliness," in *The Encyclopedia of Philosophy*, vol. 8, pp. 174–176.

38. George H. Hamilton, *Painting and Sculpture in Europe: 1880–1940* (Baltimore: Penguin Books, 1983), p. 235.

39. Deut. 7:25–26; Deut. 12:31; Deut. 13:15; Deut. 29:16. See also Deut. 18:9–12, which includes abominable practices such as passing children through the fire, divination, sorcery, animal charming, inquiring of an *ohv* or *yidoni*, and consulting the dead.

40. Deut. 17:1.

41. Lev., 11:10–13; Lev. 11:43; Lev. 20:25; Deut. 14:3.

42. Lev. 18:22; Lev. 18:26–27; Lev. 20:13; Deut. 22:5; Deut. 23:18–19; Deut. 24:4.

43. Deut. 25:16.

44. Cecil Roth, *A History of the Marranos* (New York: Meridian Books and Philadelphia: Jewish Publication Society, 1960), pp. 8 and 179.

45. Rabbi Joseph B. Soloveitchik, "Thou Shouldst Enter the Covenant of the Lord," in Pinchas H. Peli, ed., *Soloveitchik On Repentance* (New York: Paulist Press, 1984), pp. 187–227.

46. Ibid., pp. 202–206.

47. II Sam., ch. 13.

48. Soloveitchik, op. cit., pp. 195–202.

49. Peah 1:1

50. Hospers, op. cit. p. 38.

51. Prov. 3:17.

52. See the beginning of the daily morning prayer, *Bircat HaTorah.*

53. Rabbi Chaim ben Atar, *Ohr HaChaim,* Deut. 22:8.

54. Rabbi Chaim ben Atar, *Light of Life* (North Hollywood: Newcastle Publishing Co., 1986), p. 219.

55. Rabbi Abraham I. Karelitz, (Chazon Ish), Letters, 1:9. Quoted in Rabbi Shimon Finkelman, *The Chazon Ish* (Brooklyn, New York: Mesorah Publications, 1989), p. 131.

56. Dr. Samuel Rosenblatt was a rabbi in Baltimore, Maryland. He undoubtedly appreciated the beauty in Judaism, especially since he was the son of Cantor Yossele Rosenblatt. His cited remark is from one of his sermons.

EIGHT

JEWISH SOCIAL THOUGHT

S ocial philosophy deals with man as he relates to other human beings, in contrast to man as an individual. It takes account of such
subjects as the nature and origin of society and social institutions,
a person's relationship to society at large, political theory, social ideals,
law, justice, liberty, and sovereignty.

SOCIAL NATURE OF JUDAISM

While Judaism addresses the individual, "the single one," "the lonely man
of faith," it also recognizes the social nature of men and of mankind.
The Bible asserts, "It is not good for man to be alone; I will make a
fitting helper for him."[1] The talmudic epigram "Either companionship or
death"[2] clearly indicates the desirability—nay, the absolute necessity—of
sociability for the individual person. A good portion of the Bible is directed to the Jewish *people*, to the community as a whole, not simply to
each member thereof. It is unique to Jewish society that nationhood is
an integral part of Judaism, in that nationality is a component of the
peoplehood that constitutes the religious body of Israel. The people of
Israel and the Land of Israel are a part of the religion of Israel.[3]

Judaism also recognizes the rights of other societies and of other nations. Salvation is open to all righteous people, both Jew and non-Jew. "The pious among the peoples of the world have a share in the world to come."[4] The prophets delivered their messages mainly to Israel, but many of their prophesies are addressed to other people as well, with the book of Ovadiah directed exclusively to the people of Edom.[5] Of course it is not surprising that God is concerned with all people since He is a universal God, Creator of heaven and earth and all therein.

Social and political philosophy dwell largely on individual concepts and terminology. For example, Plato's *Apology* discusses the problem of political obligation and his *Republic* centers around the nature of justice. Rabbi Sol Roth (b. 1927) analyzed a number of social/political terms from a Jewish perspective. For instance, he compared the American and Jewish conceptions of freedom. To an American, freedom is a *right* pronounced in the Declaration of Independence or contractually agreed upon in the Constitution of the United States. To a Jew, freedom is a *power* associated with a historical event, namely the exodus from Egypt. What the Hebrew people acquired as a result of the departure from Egypt "was not a right, but the power to do that which it could not do in a condition of slavery. . . . For Judaism, freedom is not a right, but a power."[6] "For political democracy, freedom is an *end*. It is the purpose of the American form of government to guarantee life in freedom. Judaism's goal, however, is the embodiment within the community of a certain way of life. Freedom is merely a *means* to that end."[7]

ORIGINS OF SOCIETY AND GOVERNMENT

A question often dealt with in social philosophy is the origin of society and of government. Thomas Hobbes believed that man in the state of nature behaved like a beast while Jean-Jacques Rousseau maintained that man in his natural state is more like an angel. They both held that government was formed, if not historically, then logically, by a social contract. According to Hobbes, man cannot change the government that was created as a result of the social contract and might very well get stuck with a totalitarian, oppressive sovereign state. Both Rousseau and John Locke believed that the government provided for by the social contract can be dissolved or overthrown if it is not to the satisfaction of those being governed. How are Jewish sources similar to and different from these views of Hobbes, Locke, and Rousseau?

It would appear at first glance that Rousseau's blissful view of the past state of nature to which he would like to revert is similar to the ideal past depicted in the biblical Garden of Eden narrative. According to both, the past has been the golden age of mankind, with the ideal state having already taken place. However, we have to remember that Adam and Eve were the only humans in Eden. Their offspring and society as a whole were born and lived outside of the Garden.[8] Cain, the first born of Adam and Eve, committed homicide and fratricide when he killed his brother Abel because of jealousy. Obviously, society and social institutions, according to the Bible, did not originate in the ideal state of Paradise, despite the Garden of Eden episode. "Paradise lost" applied only to the first man and woman but not to their family and mankind as a whole, who never partook of its bliss.

ORIGINS OF THE JEWISH PEOPLE

Just as all humanity emanated from one couple, so the Jewish people finds its family tree going back to a single couple, namely Abraham and Sarah. Although they are the biological progenitors of the Israelites as portrayed by the "Treaty Between the Parts,"[9] Jews formed a people or nation after they left Egypt and accepted the Torah at Mount Sinai. Before Sinai, Jews were a family or a clan; at Sinai, they formed a community resulting from the covenant between God and Israel when the latter received the teachings and laws of the Torah.[10] Judaism teaches that an actual social contract took place in history and from it originated the social entity known as the Jewish people. Like Hobbes, Jews believe that this contract or covenant, between God and the Jewish people, is eternal and cannot be broken.

Whereas the social contract according to Hobbes might lead to irrevocable totalitarianism, the covenant at Sinai is between God and the Israelites and not between a human sovereign and his subjects. It has built-in provisions working against excessive political oppression by the ruler of the people. For one thing, the strong moral tone pervading biblical teaching applies not only to the ordinary citizen but to those in authoritative positions as well. The ruler or king is not considered above the law. He also has to study and observe the teachings of the Torah.[11] In the biblical period, if his actions were reprehensible he was subject to the rebuke of the prophets. Nathan reprimanded King David in connection with Batsheva and Uriah;[12] Elijah blasted King Ahab when the latter murdered Navot and inherited his field,[13] and Amos was undiplomatically directed by the priest Amazia to leave the Northern Kingdom of Israel because he spoke negatively about King Jereboam II and his nation.[14] It is most interesting and quite remarkable that neither Nathan nor Amos were threatened with death by the kings they rebuked. The power of the king is also checked and balanced by Jewish law. He has to share some of his authority with the high court and he can be summoned to appear before it.[15] The Jewish legal system limited the authority of the king, at least in part, because God is the true and legitimate ruler of men.

IDEAL JEWISH GOVERNMENT

Political philosophers have perennially speculated about the ideal form of government. The Bible seems to present an ambivalent approach to this subject. Upon reading Samuel's account of the excesses of a king and of the people's sinfulness in requesting one rather than relying on God,[16] we get the impression that "The government that governs least governs best," as Thomas Jefferson put it. On the other hand, the Book of Deuteronomy instructs us that when the Israelites enter their land, they are free to appoint a king to rule over them.[17] Maimonides considers the appointing of a king upon entering the Land of Israel to be one of the 613 commandments contained in the Torah.[18] As stated above, the king provided for by the Torah is not above the law but subject to it, although there is a branch of Jewish law that gives him unique authority (*Mishpat Melachim*).[19] Nevertheless, the Jewish king is more like a benevolent despot than an absolute monarch. It should also be mentioned that Don Isaac Abarbanel is an exception in Jewish political thought in that he favored republicanism over monarchy as the ideal form of government both for Jews and for other nations.[20]

Whatever the descriptions of or prescriptions for the good society delineated in Jewish sources, the utopian ideal is reserved for the future, for the Messianic era. At that time, peace will reign and everyone will seek instruction in the ways of the Lord to walk in His paths. A descendant of King David will rule with justice and equity, and harmony will prevail among all the works of creation.[21] The nature and description of the Messiah and of the Messianic Age have given rise to much speculation. There are some who envision a period of redeemed history in apocalyptic and cataclysmic terms, whereas others visualize a more tranquil, peaceful period when the highest ideals of mankind will be realized within or at the end of history. The most famous proponent of the latter conception is Maimonides. He maintained that no one is in a position to know the details of the coming of the Messiah and the Messianic times, but he wrote, "Let no one think that in the days of the Messiah any of the laws of nature will be set aside, or any innovation be introduced into creation. The world will follow its normal course."[22] He quoted the rabbinic view that "The sole difference between the present and the Messianic days is delivery from servitude to foreign powers."[23] Maimonides continued, "The sages and prophets did not long for the days of the Messiah that Israel might exercise dominion over the world.... Their aspiration was that Israel be free to devote itself to the Law and its wisdom, with no one to oppress or disturb it, and thus be worthy of life in the world to come. In that era there will be neither famine nor war, neither jealousy nor strife. Blessings will be abundant, comforts within the reach of all. The one preoccupation of the whole world will be to know the Lord."[24]

The Book of Lamentations asks God, "Why do You ignore us eternally, forsake us for so long? Bring us back to You, O Lord, and we shall return, renew our days as of old."[25] The Jewish people has a glorious past and hopes to rejuvenate its future as of yore. It seeks to renew its past and turn to God in the future in the glorious days of the Messiah. According to Judaism, "The best is yet to be."[26]

ENDNOTES

1. Gen. 2:18.

2. Taan. 23a.

3. Gen. 15:18: "On that day the Lord made a covenant with Abram, saying, 'To your offspring I assign this land.'"

4. Tosefta, San. 13.

5. Prophesies directed to non-Israelites include: Jer. 46–51, Ezek. 25–32, and Amos 1:3–2:3.

6. Sol Roth, *Halakhah and Politics* (Hoboken, NJ: Ktav Publishing House and New York: Yeshiva University Press, 1988), p. 19. Hear also Rabbi Sol Roth, "Is Judaism Democratic?" (1988), cassette tape no. 00916, available through the Rabbinic Alumni Office of Yeshiva University.

7. Ibid., p. 100.

8. According to San. 38b, Adam and Eve spent only several hours in the Garden of Eden, having sinned and been expelled during the first day of their existence.

9. Gen. 15:7–21.

10. Ex. 19:1–8; Ex. 19:16–20:14.

11. Deut. 17:18–20.

12. II Sam. 12:1–10.

13. I Kings, ch. 21.

14. Amos 7:10–12.

15. San. 19a. For an account of the nature of the monarchy in Judaism, see Maimonides, "Hilchot Melachim," which is the last section of his *Mishneh Torah*; Judah D. Eisenstein, "Melech," in his *Otzar Dinim Uminhagim* (New York: Hebrew Publishing Co., 1938), pp. 230–232; and Jacob Liver, and Louis I. Rabinowitz, "King, Kingship," in *Encyclopedia Judaica*, vol. 10, pp. 1011–1021.

16. I Sam. 7:4–22.

17. Deut. 17:14–20.

18. Maimonides, *Sefer HaMitzvot*, Positive Commandment no. 173.

19. Menachem Elon, "Mishpat Ivri," in *Encyclopedia Judaica*, vol. 12, pp. 136–137.

20. Liver and Rabinowitz, "King, Kingship," op. cit., p. 1021; See also Benzion Netanyahu, *Don Isaac Abravanel* (Philadelphia: Jewish Publication Society, 1968), pp. 173–180.

21. Is. 2:2–4 and Is. ch. 11.

22. Maimonides, *Mishneh Torah*, book 14, "Judges," 12:1, Isadore Twersky, trans., *Maimonides Reader* (New York: Behrman House, 1972), p. 224.

23. Ibid., p. 224, book 14, 12:2, San. 91b

24. Ibid., pp. 225–226 book 14, 12:3–4. For an overview of the Jewish concept of the Messiah and Messianism, see the "Messiah" entry in the *Encyclopedia Judaica*, vol. 11, pp. 1407–1416.

25. Lam. 5:20–21.

26. Robert Browning, "Rabbi Ben Ezra," Stanza 1 (poem).

INDEX

About the Author

Sheva Grumer Brun received a B.A. degree in philosophy from Brooklyn College in 1955 and a B.H.L. degree from the Seminary College of Jewish Studies in 1956. She was employed at the library of the Jewish Theological Seminary, and was an Assistant Librarian at the Stern College division of Yeshiva University. She compiled a brief bibliography for the Jewish Book Council on general reference works in English for Jewish research. Mrs. Brun resides in New York City, and has a son, a daughter-in-law, and a very young grandson.